The World to Come

Writings on Ethics and Politics

Beginning at the moment of deepest catastrophe, there exists the chance for redemption.

– *Gershom Scholem*

The World to Come

Writings on Ethics and Politics

Saitya Brata Das

AAKAR

THE WORLD TO COME

Saitya Brata Das

First Published 2015

ISBN 978-93-5002-328-0

Price: ₹ 395

Published by
AAKAR BOOKS
28 E Pocket IV, Mayur Vihar Phase I, Delhi 110 091
Phone : 011 2279 5505 Telefax : 011 2279 5641
aakarbooks@gmail.com; www.aakarbooks.com

Printed at
Sapra Brothers, New Delhi 110092

For
Munmun

Contents

PART IV: Fragments

Acknowledgements

The author thanks Teji Grover for allowing her painting to be used on the cover.

The following articles are published previously. Permission is taken to re-publish them.

1. "'To Philosophize is to Learn How to Die'?", *Kritike*, Vol. 2, No. 1, June 2008 (31-49).
2. "Philosophy and Melancholy: Benjamin on Language and Truth", a review article on Ilit Ferber's *Philosophy and Melancholy: Benjamin's Early Reflections on Theatre and Language* (Stanford: Stanford University Press, 2013), published in *Journal for Comparative and Continental Philosophy*, Vol. 6, No. 1, May 2014 (90-98).
3. "Theatre, Number, Event: An Appraisal", a review of Soumyabrata Choudhury's *Theatre, Number, Event: Three Studies on the Relationship Between Sovereignty, Power and Truth* (Shimla: IIAS, 2013), published in http://humanitiesunder ground.wordpress.com/2013/04/28/theatre-number-event-an-appraisal/.
4. "Death, Life and Law", published in issue 5, *Café Dissensus* (http://cafedissensus.com/2014/01/01/death-life-and-law/).

Introduction

I

At the heart of Jewish messianic thought there lays an idea, so succinctly expressed by Gershom Scholem in the following sentence: "Beginning at the moment of deepest catastrophe, there exists the chance for redemption". This messianic idea of redemption, expressed thus, is based upon a distinction between the unredeemed world and *the world to come*. It is fundamental to this messianic idea that this distinction can't be grasped as transition or mediation. There is no simple transition from the unredeemed world to the redemptive world of messianic fulfilment. This non-transition between these two worlds is a qualitative difference, ungraspable to the dialectical idea of synthesis that reduces the messianic intensity of difference into a quantitative difference arranged on a homogeneous scale whose unity is assured by the self-same principle of the subject. The great 19th century dialectical-historical idea of progress, irresistibly oriented towards a determinable *telos* of the movement of the world-historical politics, takes away the radicality of the messianic event of redemption arriving on the landscape of catastrophe. In this manner, such metaphysics of history turns into apologetic of what already exists as legitimate and legitimizing worldly powers in our profane order.

It is against this conformism of the world-historical politics, the messianic idea insists on the idea of redemption that radically sets the world apart from its foundation. The promise of *the world to come* is, thus, not a quantitatively different next world on a homogeneous line of the self-same, but erupting or transcendental breaking through of that which is incalculable, unforeseeable, and radically new. Such a radically new world always to come, irreducible to that which is to be achieved progressively and additively in the profane order, renders de-legitimate all the earthly sovereignties of the worldly domain. Thus *the world to come*, the redeemed world of unconditional justice, deprives the worldly orders of law and sovereignty their claim of ultimate legitimacy. The messianic idea of justice demands catastrophe of the worldly orders of law and sovereignty. *The world to come* is not the world of legitimacy and legality but the exceptional and the unconditional "to come" without sovereignty.

It is in the name of the unconditional *to come*, in the name of the un-deconstructible idea of redemption that the worldly sovereignties of the profane order are to be deconstructed. In recent philosophical thinking, this idea of messianic promise is taken out of its specific theological context, and is made it into the structural condition of opening up any discourse as such. In the irreducible *differance* of the unconditional justice and the conditioned order of law, there is to be heard the immemorial promise that opens up all futurity of sense and meaning. Such an immemorial promise, whose fulfilment opens up a radical advent of future beyond all self-presence, is the non-totalizable affirmation outside all negative and positive propositions. Each time we open our mouth, so as to speak, promise must always already—that means, immemorially—open our language, even before there is law, even before there comes to be power, even before there comes to establish worldly sovereignties on the profane order that seek our obligations. The promise of *the world to come* destitutes the worldly powers of legitimacy and legality of their claims of autochthony and sovereignty, of originary and autarchy. An immemorial beginning before the originary and an extremity of the messianic arrival *to come* with the downfall of earthly sovereignties: this messianic idea, unthinkable, is an impossible idea. Such impossibility has to do with un-doing of the entire domain of "possibilities" and "capacities", that is, the domain of law and its legitimacy, of power and its violence.

It is this difficult idea that tacitly or overly haunts my thinking and writings of the last 15 years. This book is a collection of my writings written on different occasions. They are written in different discursive registrars. There are essays; there are reviews of books written by others; there are fragments wherein thinking crystallizes itself at the moment of its arrest; and there are postscripts to my book *The Promise of Time* which was published three years ago. I would not like to impose a false unity on this collection of writings which are so different from each other in their insistence and in their interests, in their tones and in their styles. But there is a certain obsession I see—in which case I am only the first reader of my works—that runs throughout my writings for the last 13-15 years, that resonates in all my writings and thinking: that is, my insistence on the unconditional claim of the unconditioned, which I name—taking my inspiration from Jacques Derrida and Emmanuel Lévinas, from Walter Benjamin and Franz Rosenzweig, among so many others—"the advent of pure future that is always to come", the un-totalizable thinking of the event, which is nothing other than the thought of the world always to come. Hence is the title: *The World to Come.*

PART I

ESSAYS

1

Death and Immortality in Plato and Lévinas

The dominant tradition of Occidental metaphysics claims the question of being to be the most fundamental matter of thinking. Plato (or Plato's Socrates) is thus considered to be the moment when philosophy "proper" begins. Here the question of being is posed in a manner that is to determine the coming more than two thousand years of Occidental philosophical thinking. Taking up the twofold questions of death and immortality in Plato as he discusses in the dialogue *Phaedo* and relating them to the question of justice in the *Republic*, this paper attempts to read Plato again against the grain, this time in light of our contemporary ethical thinker Emmanuel Lévinas. Thus the transcendence of justice as Lévinas discusses in his works is shown to have resonated in Plato's idea of "Good beyond being". At stake is the transformation of the idea of philosophy itself which, as *Philo-Sophia*, is less concerned with the intrigue of being than with the transcendence of Good beyond being. If death is considered to be the innermost scandal of ontology—where the question is that of "to be or not to be"—then *Philo-Sophia* that is concerned with the transcendence of justice beyond law, the transcendence of Good beyond being, somehow opens death beyond its final significance. Reading Plato with Lévinas, this paper attempts to argue that the questions of immemorial (that opens us to a past beyond a *passed past*, which is the Platonic idea of *Anamnesis*) and immortality (that opens us to a future that exceeds death, and that which, while giving us hope, does not permit anticipation), which are posed at the very inception of philosophy, somehow exceeds its ontological obsession, opening us to a relation to others in an ethical mode beyond being, as expressed in the Lévinasian use of the Biblical commandment: "Thou shalt not kill".

***

Dia-Chronos

Death and immortality: an intrigue of a relation that seems to be at stake here, an intrigue from which the name or idea "philosophy" from its very inception would not have remained unaffected, untouched, unmoved. Should we be able to say, with a little more emphasis, that the idea or name *Philo-Sophia* itself from the moment of its inception—the moment that we mark with the signature of Plato—is so entangled in this tangled relation between death and immortality that the *sense* of philosophy itself *as* philosophy can even be said to have its innermost possibility derived from the relation that happens or doesn't happen between death and immortality? Death and immortality would, then, signify less that of two philosophical questions among others than that of the *sense* of philosophy itself from its innermost ground. As if philosophy can't help being fascinated by that which entangles it in turn, as in a complex plot by a secret invisibly presenting itself in every turn of events, like a detective story written by a master storyteller who dupes us in each turn of events only to disclose that which is not anticipated by the given logical chain of events. A surplus of logic, an excess of economy is at work here, intriguing us, tempting us, alluring us. Does this mean that welcoming death in the innermost heart of philosophical thinking and existing would also be its enjoyment, a philosophical enjoyment of death? As if philosophy can't help being lured into a promise of *jouissance* and thus getting entangled in an impasse that evokes in turn a law of reason condemning it as illicit or illegitimate. *Jouissance*: *la petite mort,* as they say in French. An orgiastic enjoyment of death: is this the secret that lures philosophy into an ineluctable and yet necessary entanglement? What would be the secret liaison that this discourse called "philosophy" harbours with death in such a manner that it would also be its enjoyment? Death:

is this the name of philosophy's desire? Philosophy: the orgiastic enjoyment of death? As if there is an intrigue, a secret plotting between death and desire that will be the "proper" to philosophy itself; as if to philosophize is to welcome dying while one is still alive, and hence would be its enjoyment proper to itself. As if certain pleasure or enjoyment of death would be that indelible taste that for the first time must open the text of philosophy to itself in a way that is never to be closed once. And this is so despite all insistence contrary that philosophy can indeed be brought to its closure.

If the enjoyment of death or this welcoming death is the heart of our existence and of philosophical existence in particular, how to think this plenitude of enjoyment that opens to an excess along with the other task of philosophy, namely philosophy that insists on getting drunk and yet remaining sober all the while? For is not "philosophy" also the name of that same discourse that tirelessly insists on the sober prose of measure and severity of justice, on the measure of justice that would also be the justice of measure? How, then, to think together this entangled liaison between the enjoyment of death and, on the other hand, the rigour of a justice in its tireless insistence on measure, itself without measure—the immeasurable itself? An enigma of a relation is this between *l'amor* of *la mort*, a kiss of love that is also the kiss of death on one hand, and on the other, that which is still outstanding, that which still stands out, the leftover or the remnant of a breath, which is something like a hope for immortality, which breathes in us an immortality of an immemorial hope.

Already, in the very first coupling of love and death, the unthinkable strife between them must have made itself audible and visible. Between love and death is there a relation in which each calls to the other, like two beings in love, separated from the other by an abyss of a distance, removed and un-removed at the same instance and by the same measure. The "same" of this measure is also this "other", a "sync" that is also "dia": a *dia-synchrony* that seems to be this philosophy itself—the same *separating* itself from itself, a *setting apart*, a departing of itself from the other at the "same" instance of unity, as if the instance of unity with the other and with oneself can only be the most anguished *adieu*, the most painful "farewell", a kiss of love and the kiss of death. As if each moment of welcoming the other at the heart of our existence must also the end of the world, the other's world, the world of the other. *Eros* strives with and against this *Eschaton* called *Thanatos* that unknowingly erupts in the middle of our existence, creating a void, a "dia" at the heart of any "sync" of synchrony. From this nearness of love, so immersed in the ever renewing presencing of itself, the distance of the last, namely death, is drawn near to me as I am drawn near to the other. As if in every inauguration—for love is nothing other than "inauguration" par excellence— an *adieu* is announced at the same instance, in the same voice, in the same cry of the other. In unity I am separated, in separation am I united with the other—in love and in death! Is this the meaning of the Biblical saying that goes: love is as strong as death? Isn't this equality, marked by "as" means the measure of the same *diachronic* each time, each time departing from the same, each time participating by partitioning in the depth of its immanence so that the fragility of love can be said to be as strong as the power of death? If not, then by what measure other than the measure of the same (*diachronic* each time) that the fragility of love rises up to encounter with the all powerful death? As if there is in fragility—a murmur, a humming, a rustling, a haunting melody almost fainting away, like a naked breath—that could not be completely vanquished by death, something like a remnant still outstanding or something like an immemorial touching of the invisible within the flesh of the visible. As if each instance of my life is entangled in this eternal *polemos* of love and death: loving having to die and loving not having to die each time anew and each time different.

The Inquietude of the Immemorial

Already in the Platonic dialogue *Phaedo*, the diachrony of death affects the figure of "the philosopher". There the death of the philosopher, namely Socrates, is dramatized: Socrates is the one who is departing and separating from the world, as if being a "philosopher"—the unique title of a singular being—Socrates must remain apart and solitary, singularized by his death. Isn't it what Socrates (Plato's Socrates) himself says in that unforgettable dialogue called *Phaedo*: "Those who apply themselves to philosophy in the proper way are doing no more nor less than to prepare themselves for the moment of dying and the state of death."[1] The philosopher, while existing at the heart of human community and sharing in vagaries of social existence, opens up a "dia" in the depth of its synchrony, a discontinuity in the continuum of its lived time, a disjunction in the immanence of its self-presence. His death is the event of singularity, an event raising itself against the power of the universal embodied in the Athenian State, setting him apart from the normative obligations that are demanded from him. Here is a significance of the death of a philosopher that is not exhuasted and subsumed to the meaning that the universal assigns to each of its citizens as particular ones. As though there is something in this event of death that somehow absolves itself or unbinds itself from the universality of a genus, the universality in the name of which the State can wage wars against particulars in order to subsume them under its fold. A tragic un-binding it is, if the essence of the tragic is nothing other than unbinding, while *holding*-together, not between the power of the universal against the particular but the universal with and without the singular at the same instance, a *diachrony* which is tragic.[2]

Socrates de-parts from others and from himself in an equal measure; or, even better, he brings this partition within himself at each turn of his life—the partition between his body and soul, between that which claims normative obligations from us on behalf of the existing powers of the world and on the other hand that utopian, *pneumatic* principle that affects the world of powers with a fragility and an inexorable precariousness. How to name this partitioning if not by this word "death", which is not a concept here nor a localizable and graspable state of affairs *in* the world but an event that affects the whole of existence and the world as such? Socrates therefore has to introduce this ontological void into his own life—a philosophical life that is—by the separation of principles, forces, affects, passions in an inimitable manner. A paradigm of a form of life it is, precisely because of this inimitable character, or rather where *mimesis* disrupts the memory of the origin by introducing the immemorial before origin. A philosophical life, the life of Socrates: an incessant departure from the given, an infinite setting apart in life from within life, to welcome the utopia of the other in place of "self" or "ego". As though to live a philosophical life means *always already* to prepare for farewell, or to wish for God's blessing: *Adieu.*

"To-God": mark the infinitive of the verbal wherein the excess of the future must always already announce itself in all self-presence, something like a surplus or an infinite that is at one and yet separate from time that *presents*. Hence is the necessity of "preparation", preparation for what always already and yet that which is always "to come". "To come": this idea of God or the idea of "immortality" is the idea of *God to come*, or the idea of immortality to arrive. The infinite idea, or the idea of the infinite is this immortality, which—while it has always been from time immemorial—is still *not yet*: an outstanding future, *utopia* which means a place not yet, *u-topos*. In the dialogue of *Phaedo* which is conducted on the day of the death of the philosopher, discussion thus inevitably goes from the idea of the immemorial to immortality, as if the opening of temporality from the heart of finitude needs simultaneous opening to the immemorial as well as immortality. Socrates must prepare— thus must pass through the destitution of death—for what is *to come*, but what comes, in a way, must *always already* be an immemorial past, before the past that can arrive to my memory. Only an immemorial *comes*, not in the sense of that which comes to pass by, but that which is *to come* always, namely, immortality. Waiting, while preparing for this arrival —and to "live" a "philosophical life" is to have time—is to prepare for *u-topia* to come. But this waiting for that which while coming, does not come to pass away, is to wait without anticipating "anything". Immortality to come is "no-thing": one can't, after all, anticipate any—"thing" in immortality at all. But one can hope, at the threshold of mortality, for what doesn't radically belong to "sync" of a life governed by a "common" *nomos* in the general order of denomination. The hope for immortality in this dialogue of Plato signifies: to hope for and yet anticipating nothing . Immortality is an affair of hope without anticipation, a hope for the radically heterogeous, incalculable eruption of immortality at the heart of existence which is always a surplus, like the surplus of the future to come without having to pass by. It is a radical "dia", this idea of immortality, where the privative "im" of "immortality" would have more than a mere negative sense in respect to "mortality". "Immortality" is not immortality of some "thing", so immortality does not have to be an act of negation of mortality. Immortality would then bear a sense not negative enough, or more than mere negation: the "otherwise" of hope, the otherwise of "utopia", the otherwise than presence or essence of a thing as facts of the world, otherwise than negativity that displays as the sovereign power of the worldly order. It is, in another word, an *event*.

Where is that immortality to be searched and found?: nowhere and everywhere, at each turn of the mortal life, at each instance of the philosophical life. At each turn of the mortal life that principle of hope is to be recovered and discovered anew. Yet this calls for preparation or education, preparation in dying, preparation to disjoin the "utopos" of immortality from the closure of *topos*, to release and free the redemptive event of futurity from the enclosures of time by separating and introducing the ontological void at the very heart of the world. To make the world fragile and precarious once more, to render the powers of the world weak and destitute once more, to loosen the grasp of sovereign-normative obligation once more: that is the task of a philosophical life. Dying would have for Socrates the sense of an opening to immortality by de-potentiating the powers of the world, by impoverishing the forces of the law in the name of a hope beyond anticipation, a hope for the unhoped for, namely justice itself—an idea of immortality from which the sense of an infinitude would not be separable.

There must thus be something spectral, utopian, ahistoricality or even a sort of transcendence about justice. Not only in the *Republic* but also in *Phaedo* the question of justice remains fundamental to the discussion. Like the soul haunting the body, justice haunts, dislocates, interrupts the orders of law founded upon sovereign powers of the world. As though, as it were, justice has to pass through or traverse through a dying by separating the world from its foundation, to appear in its inapparition: an apparition enigmatic and paradoxical, of which Plato gives the name "invisible" in *Phaedo,* which, as the pure life of the visible, is irreducible to the visible. This Platonic heterogeneity must have rent asunder all "monism" of the visible[3] and all monotheism and nomotheism of worldly sovereignty. Like a spectre, utopian the justice haunts the closures of the world from the very depth of the world, equalizing the depth of the world with its abyss. The idea of justice therefore must pass through this passage of death. In a certain passage of the *Republic*, to his interlocutor who complains that the justice that Socrates advocates is not to be found in the world, Socrates responds in the following manner: sure, justice is indeed not to be found *in* the world; it does not belong, as a spectre doesn't belong, to the world. It is not a fact among facts, a world among worlds or a presence among presences in the world; but there is no world—the world where human sociability can be conceived and lived through, the world where the political opening of each being towards the other even to be possible—without an opening to the infinitude of justice, without a transcendence towards justice, which, even if it does not permit anticipation, must allow hope for us, as it were a hope for immortality whose measure must exceed all the measures that exist as given to us: the measure of the world and the measure of time, the measure of law and the measure of the concept. It must be the measure of a transcendence not founded on the conditional in turn, a measure without the self-sameness of monism wherein the concept will be equivalent to being that it signifies. As an unconditional demand, the spectre of justice—utopian and ahistorical— haunts the body and life of the philosopher with a responsibility: this is the philosopher dying to hope, to hope that passes through the dying of the philosopher at each turn of his life, at each instance of his existence, like a *diachrony* that interrupts the continuum of *synchrony*.

Here is, then, an understanding of death that is not merely a particular event erupting at the conclusion of a life that rounds off the voyage of life. Rather the intrigue of death opens existence, which is here a philosophical existence, to the infinitude of a hope for the event of surprise that is immortality or justice. In *Phaedo* the idea of transcendence, that is immortality, is considered the event that surprises us at the limit of expectation. Is this also not the very movement of desire peculiar to philosophical life that marks it as essentially erotic? The erotic movement that constantly transcends itself—as Plato graphically evokes in his two dialogues, *Phaedrus* and *Symposium*—is this movement opening to the infinitude from the very heart of the finite. A longing for this not-yet-reached-immortality must have already inscribed itself in each throbbing of the heart of the world. An immemorial presencing itself in each throbbing of the heart of the world without ever becoming memorial in turn; an incorporealization occurring in each *corpus* of life; immortality *setting apart* mortality from its enclosures: such is the movement philosophy must introduce into the world. A movement that is irreducible to a homogeneous line of continuuity; hence, strictly speaking it is no "movement", but an arrestation of time, a standing still of time, a "dia" which is also a "sync": such is transcendence of justice in respect to law, the soul in respect to *corpus*. It does not have to be an end of time, as if time were a scale constantly pointing towards a conclusive moment; for, then, there won't be immortality either. It is rather the task of welcoming the immemorial *hic et nunc* at each instance of my life, to be hospitable to the immortality at the very heart of mortality, in the manner that invisible trembling as the life of the visible.

Hence Socrates who is preparing to die is, in a certain sense, always already *dying*; he is always already incorporealizing his *corpus*, always already opening himself to the immemorial. Immortality, according to this mode, would ceaselessly *affect* us while we are still alive, affecting us with a responsibility so inexorable and unconditional that it introduces an inquietude that never ceases with the breath of time. It is *affection* par excellence. It appears as though every corpus of human life is affected with incorporealization; each memorial event of human history is affected by the immemorial; and each mortal life is affected with immortality, by a breath of eternity—by an affection whose measure is none other than the immeasurable measure of infinitude. It is this infinitude, affecting our finite ground of existence, passes through and passes beyond death, rendering the powers of the world inoperative and insufficient. The inquietude of justice gives to me, passing through this passage of death, nothing more than the insufficiency of law and non-sovereignty of all that claims from me normative obligations on behalf of those powers that exist in the world.

Despite this hope of immortality, mourning however is not absent in *Phaedo*. Mourning all the more affects us precisely by being "absent". Plato withdraws from this spectacle of death that evokes such unconsolable mourning at the heart of the Athenian community. Socrates asks his disciple to drive away the women who are ceaselessly mourning and Apollodorus could not be consoled. "He weeps beyond measure", as Lévinas says. Here is a mourning that affects the whole Platonic dialogue, an affection that goes beyond "the splendour of being", an excess of emotion in encountering the death of the other[4]. For Lévinas, responsibility understood as this inexorable opening to the other, begins here: in this intrigue of death wherein the death of the other doesn't have to begin and end with the "self", or with "being" riveted back into itself.

Transcendance of Justice

Death—the intrigue of philosophy? If this intrigue can't be reduced to an understanding of it on the basis of the question of self; or, if such an intrigue can't be cleared up in the luminosity of being, then the intrigue that is at stake here is not merely an intrigue of philosophy or a philosophical intrigue but an intrigue *for* philosophy. A "scandal of philosophy", in the manner of the Lévinasian saying. It is the intrigue that points this discourse called "philosophy" to its limit without enabling philosophy to attain its closure once and for all. Rather it shows the impossibility of the closure of philosophy, and hence is its "scandal" character, its "poisonous sting".[5] Perhaps this discourse called "philosophy", intrigued by death, has never reached this closure in its history. Despite the "splendour of being" displayed, there is a transcendence that Lévinas finds in Plato's *Phaedo* wherein lies the true intrigue of death, death that can't be understood as mere negation or annihilation, death that doesn't have to participate in "the epic of being", but a death "from which time takes all its patience"[6] wherein certain passivity is emphasized and which escapes the intentionality of a self. Here time is not understood on the basis of death nor the significance of death receives exhuastion in the meaning that is assigned to it for the role it plays in this "epic of being", but rather otherwise: death on the basis of time wherein time opens to the infinitude of future coming from its extremity. An eschatology, if one would like to say. Lévinas finds in this understanding the very possibility of responsibility to the other. Contra Heidegger's understanding of death as "the possibility of impossibilities" wherein a sense of capacity or even a sense of mastery is unmistakably present, Lévinas emphasizes here a death that marks the other with an irreducible fragility, evoking an emotion, an affection, a ceaseless mourning equal to no measure of being. An "impossibility of possibilities" it is, that is the trauma of subjectivity torn open to the other in responsibility. The other, the figure of weakness, evokes an affection which is not anxiety before one's own death that is proper to "me" and that would be finally appropriated. In this manner, Lévinas opens up the idea of the infinitude understood as responsibility to the other's irreplaceable death that introduces the "dia" into the "chronos" of "mine", a *diachrony* that is a deference to the unknown, a departure to the point of no return, a separation without returning to appropriation. It is grief or a mourning never assuaged and never converted into the meaning of being or into the possibility of signification. It is affection of mourning and not anxiety before a death that is each time "mine" in the sense that Heidegger understood by the term *Jemeinigkeit*. Here is the idea of an intrigue from which philosophy would receive for Lévinas the unique and unsurpassable name "ethics". Not that ethics has to replace philosophy or surpass philosophy, for philosophy at its very inception is intrigued by the ethical, given in the idea of transcendence or infinitude, an idea that passes through and passes beyond death; or, even better, the very idea of philosophy itself, in its insistence on the Platonic "Good beyond being", always already is ethical in its essential self-understanding. It is the Good itself that has always already cleared the space for even the intelligibility of being to take place. Hence this Good is the third, being "before" of the coupling of being and its nothing, irreducible to the intrigue that being entangles itself with this nothing.

The intrigue that Lévinas has in mind here, the intrigue that receives the name "ethical" for him, the intrigue that intrigues us, intricates us, entangles us, weaves us into, is the plot wherein subjectivity is implicated in an accusation and thus is guilty in confronting the unconditional commandment: "thou shalt not kill". A commandment and not a law: Lévinas here rigorously follows Rosenzweig's distinction between "commandment" (*Gebot*) and "law" (*Gesetz*). The ethical prohibition of killing is a *Gebot* and not *Gesetz*. This is a fundamental distinction crucial to Lévinas' ethical thinking. This *diachrony* of the inexpiable guilt, insofar as it increases more and more I am responsible to the other, can only be considered in relation to the *Gebot* wherein the infinitude of the unconditional announces itself in the mode of a prohibition: "Thou shalt not kill". The transcendence of commandment in respect to law lies in the justice that adheres in it, which is not yet established and which can't be established to the measure of law. It is this deference and difference of justice that opens up the closure of being from its intrigue to the other intrigue wherein "I", the survivor, can't assume itself without always already responding to the address coming from the other who is dying, who is hungry and destitute, abandoned to utter nakedness and powerlessness.

Death remains an intrigue for me insofar as it constantly calls me into question by announcing a prohibition in the language of commandment: "Thou shalt not kill". It thus, in *a priori* manner, calls into question all violence emanating from the light of being. It is a judgment, not of law but of commandment, on the violence of history: one can't kill the other, the other alone whom I would like to destroy. In encountering the other's death, I am intricated in the intrigue of responsibility which is the intrigue of the infinite itself, a transcendence without measure, the immeasurable immemorial that can't be deduced from the worldly measure of fact or presence. It is the event of the world for me.

In Excess: Good Beyond Being

We have thus seen in the Platonic "Good beyond being", and in the Biblical commandment "Thou shalt not kill" two modes of opening to an excess that is without being, that excess whose existence is not determined in turn by the law of being. Not having to emanate from its dialectical counterpart, Good is not opposed to evil (or bad); in the same (not identical way) way "thou shalt not kill" does not emanate from the gaze of law. They emanate from the other source; or, better, they are themselves the other origin. For Plato, this is the moment when the whole process of dialectics itself comes to a standstill in a moment of astonishment or marvel; as if, this inapparition making itself apparent, or the invisible making itself visible without being "visible", must arrest the continuous process of reason. There is thus in Plato something otherwise than "know thyself"; or, rather, in "know thyself" itself there announces something that is otherwise than the intelligibility of being. This Good is the immemorial "before" and an affair of the immortality "after", a transcendence of justice that destitutes in advance each attempt at instituting worldly sovereignty on the basis of nomothetic operation. It is this philosophical worklessness that is the scandal for Athenian democracy. It is this immemorial that is the scandal, the unbearable and monstrous operation that Socrates unleashed at the heart of Athenian society.

In Lévinas, on the other hand, this scandal announces itself in a commandment that prohibits, but prohibits in a way distinguished from the prohibition emanating from the locus of law. This difficulty of thinking—a scandal—of a categorical imperative without being regulated by the ideal of reason is trauma, a vertigo of thought. The immemorial traumatizes me, but also releases me beyond being to the Good which is the immemorial, each time introducing an inquietude at the heart of my memory. In each case, death is never final and never at the service of the intelligibility of being. In each case, death is denuded of its final significance for us. In the nudity of dying, immortality appears—without appearing—as hope for the still outstanding, justice that is still left over, a remnant of time not yet finished.

NOTES

1. Plato, "Phaedo," in *The Trial and Execution of Socrates*, trans. Peter George (London: The Folio Society, MCMLXXII, 1972), p. 103.
2. Reiner Schürmann, *Broken Hegemonies*, trans. Reginald Lily (Bloomington: Indiana University Press, 2003).
3. Michel Henry, *The Essence of Manifestation*, trans. Girard Etzkorn (Martinus Nijhoff, 1973).
4. Emmanuel Lévinas, *God, Death and Time,* trans. Bettina Bergo (Stanford, California: Stanford University Press, 2000), p. 18.
5. Franz Rosenzweig, *The Star of Redemption*, trans. Barbara Galli (Madison, Wisconsin: University of Wisconsin Press, 2004), p. 9.
6. Emmanuel Lévinas, *God, Death and Time*, trans. Bettina Bergo (Stanford, California: Stanford University Press, 2000), p. 7.

2

Ereignis: *Heidegger on Art, Technology and Metaphysics*

I

What I would attempt to do today is something much more modest than what I originally proposed myself to do. Instead of grappling with the Heideggerian idea of *Ereignis* or the event of appropriation in itself and in its light raising the questions concerning art, technology and metaphysics in their innermost relationship, I would rather present to you a few hints or indications which will prepare us to understand what Heidegger attempted to think with this difficult name *Ereignis,* perhaps the most difficult of Heideggerian ideas in his entire works. The name *Ereignis* itself is only a hint or beckoning: *Ereignis* beckons us and in this manner exposes us towards that what remains unthought and unthinkable within metaphysics, and that can only arrive to us, in a momentary manner, like a flash of lightning. *Ereignis*, which the English translators translate as "the event of appropriation", is the event of arrival to which concealment is "proper" to it as much as its unconcealment. In other words, the event of this arrival or this arrival of the event is an agonal-tragic *belonging*-together of a polemical difference of concealment and unconcealment. The event of appropriation is *belonging*-together of a tragic dissonance of concealment and unconcealment. We don't know the date and time of the arrival of this event of appropriation; it does not belong to our destinal historical knowledge. This is so because such and such historical destiny must already be sent to us beforehand by such an event of arrival. Where such knowledge is lacking, we must learn to listen and receive the hints. This is the famous Heideggerian idea of *Wink*— hinting or beckoning—an idea that Heidegger propounds as early as *Being and Time*. In this early book, Heidegger thinks *Wink* phenomenologically: the gesture that Heidegger releases free here under the name of "phenomenology" is itself the gesture of hinting towards that which can't be considered within traditional ontology. What phenomenalizes itself in this *Wink* is none other than Being itself. Such hinting can't be thought of within the propositional structure of metaphysics. Therefore the Heideggerian phenomenology must pass through deconstruction or *Destruktion* of classical ontology. If we want to understand today the idiomatic and singular Heideggerian thoughts on art and technology, it would then be necessary to understand the peculiar way or the singular path through which metaphysics would undergo its destitution or deconstruction in his thought. For Heidegger, the questions concerning technology and art must now be decisively posed in relation to and outside metaphysics. This means: from the task of thinking outside the propositional structure of metaphysics. This entails a task of thinking and poetizing that hints or beckons, each in its singular manner, towards the other inauguration when metaphysics comes to a sudden halt. Therefore poetizing and thinking is outside metaphysics; or, should we be able to say that in an essential sense, there is no thinking and poetizing within metaphysics. Metaphysics has forgotten poetizing and thinking: such oblivion has determined the history of beings, that is metaphysics, for more than two thousand years. Such poetizing is to be distinguished from what we have come to call "aesthetics" as the discourse or the "science of the beautiful". In a similar but in a different way, thinking is not the innermost concern of representational or propositional structure of metaphysics. The questions concerning art and technology must then be understood in light of the question concerning the overcoming of metaphysics. Heidegger's enigmatic phrase that the question concerning technology is itself *not* itself technical or technological receives now a clarity: the question concerning technology is not in itself technological but metaphysical; it is the question concerning the whole discourse called "metaphysics" as such, the discourse that understands beings on the ground of Being, or Being as the ground of beings.

With this preliminary remark, let me pose now more clearly what I am attempting today. I will read with you Heidegger's famous 1935 lecture called *The Origin of the Work of Art* in order to prepare ourselves to confront the questions concerning art and technology. Nothing original or new will be attempted in this preliminary attempt; far from it, my attempt is only to make visible, as much as possible here, these Heideggerian questions once again, so as to pose these questions for ourselves, important and decisive questions that they are for us.

II

First of all, let's ponder on the question of "origin", one of the keywords in this lecture called *Origin of the Work of Art*, appearing as it is in the very title of the lecture. In a way, for us, the Heideggerian use of the word "origin", here as elsewhere, appears nothing less than a "scandal", for what is more metaphysical than this questioning of "origin"? If the Heideggerian task of thinking consists of destitution or deconstruction of metaphysics, then asking the origin of the phenomenon called art or technology itself would make such a questioning belonging to that very metaphysics that is to be subjected to deconstruction. However, the German word that Heidegger uses for origin, *Ürsprung*, is opened up to say something fundamentally different: *Ür-* which means "primordial" and *Sprung*—which means "leap", hints at the idea of origin as a primordial leaping forth. The origin, by taking the leap, opens up the world in its struggle with the earth. As such, the word "origin" is another name for the event that we are speaking of as *Ereignis*: the origin is the clearing-opening of the arrival which is to come. The notion of origin, then, is not to be understood as a metaphysical nostalgia of Heidegger to recover a remote original past, but rather to be understood as the leap out of metaphysics and clearing-opening for the arrival from the extremity of the future, which he names as *Ereignis*. That the origin opens up the world and that it opens up the world in a manner that is in the agonal- tragic strife with the earth implies an essential dissonance of the origin. In the name *Ereignis* which is the event of appropriation, one must also hear the other trait of expropriation. In the same way, in the world-disclosure of the origin we must also hear resonance of the other trait, the concealment or withdrawal of the earth. The origin, then, is the open space where there takes places the strife of the world and earth: the un-concealing-opening and concealing-withdrawing thus belong together as two dissonant tragic-agonal traits of the origin wherein truth happens or occurs. Such tragic-agonal belonging together of concealment-unconcealment is to be heard in the Heideggerian name for truth, *Aletheia*: non-truth, that is, the oblivion, *lethe* from which truth is to be wrested away, *A-letheia.*

The work of art is the happening of this truth, the occurrence of *Aletheia*. Heidegger here attempts to think this truth, *Aletheia*, in a more originary manner than truth understood as *adaequatio*, the propositional truth of predication based on the adequacy of subject and its object, of subject and its predicate, as though the propositional structure of a statement must mirror the very structure of the thing itself. The truth of poetizing—for poetizing here is considered as what is essential to art as such—this truth of poetizing or poetizing of truth (*Aletheia)* can't be thought of within the predicative propositional structure of truth (*adaequatio*) in metaphysics. As such, the work of art can't be thought of primarily as an object of *aisthesis*, an object of "sensuous apprehension", an object of aesthetic experience that the discourse called "aesthetics" is concerned with. As happening of truth, that is, opening of the world in its strife with the withdrawing earth, so says Heidegger: "Art is considered neither an area of cultural achievement nor an appearance of spirit; it belongs to the *Ereignis* by way of which the "meaning of Being" can alone be defined"[1].

Now this is important for us to consider. Art can be reduced neither to the idea of cultural achievement nor to the Hegelian idea of art as an expression of the absolute subject; art is to be reduced neither to an object of aesthetic experience nor to the predicative structure of the logical proposition. Thus the notion of culture as much as the aesthetic experience that the modern man today cherishes and enjoys, the notion of the subject as much as the predicative structure of propositional truth that technology presuppose and are founded upon, belong to the innermost transmutations within the epochal history of beings that Heidegger names as "metaphysics". On the other hand, the work of art whose essential nature is poetizing, belongs to the other inauguration outside metaphysics, since now the history of beings has become epochal, that means, "finished, dated and terminated".[2] Poetizing then belongs, not to metaphysics, but to *Ereignis*, than to that other inception outside the epochal closure of metaphysics.

It is in this context, that the Heideggerian question concerning technology is to be understood. The Greek word *Techne* means nothing technological; it means neither craftsmanship nor a calculable taking possession of any phenomena that we encounter in the world by inscribing them within a means-end relationship of instrumentality. It rather means, as Heidegger reminds us, "a mode of knowing" that "*brings forth* present beings as such beings *out of* concealedness and specifically *into* the unconcealedness of their appearance".[3] If the artist is also called by the Greek *technites* as much as the craftsman, it is because there occurs in them a "bringing forth and presenting that causes beings in the first place to come forward" in the midst of the being that grows out of its own accord, *Phusis*"[4] . To create a work of art means to fix this happening of truth in "figure", in *Gestalt*. The verb *Stellen* means *placing*: the en-framing character of *Gestalt* lets truth to *take place* in the Open wherein the fourfold of beings—the divine and mortals, world and earth—"come forward and be present in assuming an appearance"[5].

In his essays that address the question concerning technology, Heidegger uses this expression *Gestell* as a key to the nature of modern technology. The essence of technology is *Gestell* or Enframing: modern technology arranges, orders, sets in place, in sum en-frames phenomena, including man himself, as calculable entities. But this sense of *Gestell* is derived from *Poiesis* that is to be understood as letting beings come to presence out of unconcealment. *Poiesis* is a singular mode of the happening of truth understood as *Aletheia*. In that sense, the originary essence of technology is, in itself, nothing technological; it is rather the extreme epochal fulfilment of the destiny of the history of being wherein the originary *Aletheia* has undergone oblivion. The essence of technology as *Gestell*, "which now means in commandeering everything into assured availability" and thus "taking control of the absolute"[6] is the most extreme forgetting of the originary eruption of truth as *Aletheia*. The essence of technology is then metaphysics thorough and thorough, grounded upon the metaphysics of the subject, the same metaphysics expresses itself in still another manner as "aesthetics", the discourse that determines the works of art as an essentially aesthetic expression of the absolute subject.

Therefore in Heidegger's deconstruction of the epochal constitution of metaphysics has to raise the question concerning art and technology at the same time. At the epochal closure of that metaphysics—when metaphysics has become "epochal", dated and finished, fulfilled and terminated—art as poetizing now can be seen as grounding or founding of truth, a new inauguration outside metaphysics, by taking the leap of the origin (*Ürsprung*). In other words, the founding of truth leaps, and incepts a new beginning. Art now, released from the totalizing metaphysics of the Subject, opens the Open wherein the mortal and the divine, the world and the earth—the fourfold—each comes into its own, to what is "proper" to itself and at the same time each one opening to the other. At the closure of metaphysics, it is this poetizing and thinking that opens the possibility of *Gespräch* or this conversation of the fourfold. Such poetizing can neither be understood as expression of the human Subject nor as a cultural treasure of a particular autochthonous people, but sheltering-welcoming of the Open wherein each of the folds, in respect to the others, may come to its own.

Seeing from the Heideggerian perspective, then, the idea of "post-humanism" or "trans-humanism" that we talk about and celebrate today and which is supposed to have been inaugurated by unthinkable acceleration of technology—is not only profoundly mistaken but confusing to the extreme. The planetary domination of technology in today's world is only an extreme manifestation of the metaphysics of the Subject that objectivises everything, wherein a certain metaphysical determination of "man"—a certain "humanism"—triumphs. This humanism, which in its essence metaphysical—insofar as every "humanism" is grounded upon metaphysics[7]—is based upon a certain determination of man as "producer". The metaphysical conception of labour is constitutive of this humanism, of which technology is the most extreme manifestation whose essence is *Gestell* (*En-Framing*). But this modern, technological essence as *Gestell* is not the same as the earlier Greek notion of *Gestell* as the figure that opens up the world for the fourfold, the truth, to happen in the work of art.

It is poetizing and thinking, as the two neighbouring linguistic ways of existence, that open us to a new inauguration outside the planetary technological domination and exercise of man's sovereign mastery. The way of language, language as *Wink*—that is, poetizing-language and language-thinking—abandons and renounces all mastery and all appropriation, that means, abandons the language of metaphysics itself. Since in all renunciation and abandonment there lies melancholy, all profound thinking and all great poetry is essentially melancholic, even when they speak of joy. But this melancholy is neither pessimism nor depression, but one that is joyous, for such thinking thanks to the arrival of unthought. This is so insofar there lies a *thanking* in all essential *thinking* and in all essential gratitude lies a profound joy at one with mournfulness.[8]

NOTES

1. Martin Heidegger, "The Origin of the Work of Art" in *Poetry, Language, Thought*, trans. Albert Hofstadter (Harper & Row, 2001), p. 85.
2. Reiner Schürmann, *Heidegger on Being and Acting: From Principles to Anarchy* (Indiana University Press, 1987), p. 5.
3. Martin Heidegger, "The Origin of the Work of Art" in *Poetry, Language, Thought*, trans. Albert Hofstadter (Harper & Row, 2001), p. 57.
4. Ibid., pp. 57-8.
5. Ibid., p. 58.
6. Ibid., p. 83.

7. Martin Heidegger, "Letter on Humanism" in *Pathmarks*, trans. William McNeill (Cambridge University Press, 1998), p. 245.
8. Martin Heidegger, *What is Called Thinking?*, trans. J. Glenn Gray (Harper & Row, 1976).

3

'To Philosophize is to Learn How to Die'?

> *Those who apply themselves to philosophy in the proper way are doing no more nor less than to prepare themselves for the moment of dying and the state of death.* –*Plato*.[1]

I

Philosophical thinking, as it is thinking of existence, is essentially finite thinking. This is to say that as thinking of existence, philosophical thinking is essentially *also* thinking of finitude. This 'also' is not the accidental relationship between existence and finitude. Rather, to think existence in its finitude, insofar as existence is finite, is to think existence in its existentiality. Philosophy that gives itself the task of thinking of the relationship between existence and finitude, must in the same gesture, be concerned with its own finitude: to philosophize is not only to think the finitude of existence, but the very finitude of thinking that thinks finite existence. To philosophize is not only to philosophize the finitude of existence as such, but also insofar as philosophizing itself is a task which is essentially in itself finite. To assume as the task of thinking the finitude of existence is to think the very finitude of philosophical thinking: this is the profound relationship that exists between existence and philosophy, which is that philosophizing existence and an existential philosophy are essentially finite. This is perhaps what Socrates says of philosophizing: 'To philosophize is to learn how to die.' "To philosophize is to learn how to die": this is to say, to philosophize is to learn that philosophy and existence are essentially finite. Philosophy and existence belong to finitude and gifts of finitude; therefore to philosophize is to learn how existence is this gift. To be able to learn how existence is this gift of finitude, to be able to assume this gift that makes existence essentially finite, which is to be able to assume existence at all, is to be able to die. 'Learning to die' then comes to signify the ability of dying, which is in the same gesture, the ability of existing: existence, and dying at the end must be this *ability*, of existing and dying. Philosophizing must provide, then, the learning of this ability: to be capable of death and existence. To be capable of death is to master it, to be equal to or master death, it thereby means to be immortal, to be able not to die, to be capable of immortality; by learning to die, by learning to be capable of death, we become capable of not-dying, or of immortality. To learn to die is to learn how not to die.

Yet there may be, at the same time, another thought of finite thinking, that existence and its finitude eludes the very grasp of philosophical thinking; that it marks the very limit of what came to be determined as philosophy; that in the very attempt to think existence and finitude, philosophical thinking exhausts its resources and thus is delivered over to its own finitude. Therefore the task of philosophical thinking is finite each time, which is to say, to come to face what disavows philosophical thinking, what abandons it to its finitude. This would have then another meaning of what Socrates names as *death: not the mastery of death, and not the profit of immortality, but to be abandoned to its limit, to disappear without profit and gain of immortality, to be abandoned to its finitude insofar as finitude itself eludes the mastery of philosophical thinking.* To philosophize would then be the non-mastery of dying and the experience of the gift of finitude at the limit, which means, not to be able to experience finitude, not to be able to know death so as to profit from it. If 'to philosophize is to learn how to die,' this is to say in the same gesture, to philosophize is to fail death ineluctably, to fail to realize its own finitude, in not able to *own* its own finitude and in not to be able to master death. In philosophizing, one does not learn enough of dying, if philosophy is nothing but learning to die, for to grasp death in philosophical learning is to fail death, to lose it ineluctably, to miss it and be thrown outside of it. Therefore, philosophical thinking, in the very task of thinking finitude, remains an evasion of death and a vain consolation.

What of existence then that remains for philosophy if the unthought of finitude marks the very finitude of philosophical thinking? Thinking that assumes for its task to think existence itself, therefore, always invariably led to ask the question concerning the very finitude of philosophy, which is the question of the non-appropriability of the condition of philosophizing itself, the non-appropriability of its own origin, as if, as it were, philosophy can not posit its own origin in its immanence, but for that reason, attracted, in its finitude, to the 'outside' of the groundless, the *abgrund* ground of it, which is not the negativity but groundless that exceeds all the manner grounding, thinking, positing. What is non-appropriable but existence, in its finitude, the non-posited affirmation beyond negativity and positing: such finitude, the non-posited groundless ground is the very condition of a thinking that posits, outside the negativity of the Concept, that remains excessive to being conditioned and appropriated; which is to say, with Schelling,[2] *the ground remains separated from existence* that marks the melancholy of all finite beings. In not being able to appropriate its condition, thus of its finitude, as the veil of melancholy that separates ground from existence: this finitude alone enables to have any relationship to existence at all that philosophy attempts to think, that is to *learning how to die*, which is also to say, to learn how to exist. 'To philosophize is to learn how to die' would then mean—not the mastery of death, but to learn that philosophizing is essentially that which has its non-appropriable condition outside it, hence its finitude and there alone is its freedom, a melancholic, abysmal freedom. Here I refer to a reading of Schelling's most beautiful treatise on human freedom where he elaborated this innermost connection between finitude and freedom, of melancholy of all finite beings and the joy of creating, so as to think anew freedom as finite and philosophy's relation to this joyous freedom. There alone, where finitude grants the gift of thinking lies its joy and hope, not separated from the melancholy that adheres to our finite existence, but a melancholy that is transfigured into joy, into the very possibility of creating at all. Yet that demands that we are abandoned to our own finitude, that is to say, abandoned to infinite: such an experience, says Schelling (quoted by Heidegger here) Plato, is akin to death:

> He who wishes to place himself in the beginning of a truly free philosophy must abandon even God. Here we say: who wishes to maintain it, he will lose it; and who gives up, he will find it. Only he has come to the ground of himself and has known the whole depth of life who has once abandoned everything, and has himself been abandoned by everything. He for whom everything disappeared and who saw himself alone with the infinite: a great step, which Plato compared to death.[3]

The possibility of a free beginning for philosophical thinking lies in this abandonment, being abandoned by everything and everyone, himself abandoning everything and everyone, a step of death: thus not the mastery of death, but being abandoned to the non-appropriable and to the unconditional, having to lose death while having to die, in having to miss its finitude while being delivered over to its finitude, in its incessantly being thrown over to its death and yet having to survive itself, which is to say, not being capable of death. It misses death, that is to say, it misses its condition, such is the non-condition of abandonment—for what is to philosophize but philosophize existing and dying—and yet, in missing mastering existence and dying, this alone enables philosophy to have any relationship of free beginning with existence and finitude at all. This is the profoundest ambiguity of philosophy, the very ambiguity of its possibility and existence. In its inability of death, in not being able to have the relationship with death, in not looking at death directly at the face, by looking away and averting its gaze, by taking away the poison of death's bite and yet being abandoned, precisely in this way, to abandonment: this alone is the possibility of thinking death, and the only possibility for philosophy and thinking. Rather this is the very condition of philosophy: to survive death, to escape it, or to go beyond it, to fall outside it or transcend it. Therefore philosophical thinking, that is learning to die, is at heart, but learning how to survive death and to be able to make a leap of transcendence beyond death. Socrates' rumination on philosophizing as learning to die is therefore inescapably bound up with the question of the immortality of the soul: philosophizing seems to be meaningful only to the extent that existence is not mere tarrying with death, but to transcend it so as to come back resurrected, survived, and immortal. To philosophize is in this sense is nothing but learning how to be immortal, or better, learning not to be mortal, to refuse finitude, to disavow death's poisonous breath. Philosophy, having to think finitude, having to be profited from it, having to have the relation with existence and finitude, remains disavowal of death and existence. To desire this immortality is not the mastery of death, but the very limit of philosophical thinking. Hence, existence in its finitude somehow remains unthought, unlived, impossible for philosophical thinking insofar as philosophical thinking assumes in the dominant form of tradition as metaphysics, the prima philosophy, or at its accomplishment and closure the name *Logic,* discourse of pure thought that in thinking thought also claims to think existence, so that *being* and *thought* are one.

II

'To philosophize is to learn how to die': with this Plato intimates the innermost connection between philosophy and finitude, of philosophy as essentially finite thinking. Yet finitude and death remain the innermost scandal of philosophy, scandal that is not imposed in an accidental manner from outside, but (de) constitutes the very attempt to think existence philosophically, that is to say, finitely. Yet this attempt to think existence in its finitude, in that it is, the 'facticity' of existence, the facticity of existence remains dirempted from the very thinking insofar as thinking must endeavour to grasp existence, *essentially*, in this very facticity. To learn to exist and learn to die insofar as it is to learn to grasp existence in its finitude is to hold existence in all its facticity, as it were, existence is beheld in front of the immobility of the philosopher's empty gaze, a gaze that does not waver and oscillate, that remains resolute and decisive, transfixed and transfiguring the modes of existing and dying, the vicissitudes of arriving and passing away, but itself not moved by what is gazed, resolute not to mourn what is lost without return and what is lapsed beyond the recuperative labour of memory. Therefore philosophical thinking has this innermost relationship with what Plato calls *anamnesis*: transfixation and transfiguration of existence and accomplishment of existence through this transfiguring work of *anamnesis.* Memory, the labour of transfiguration of existence, is thus nothing but a certain accomplishment, philosophically, of existence. 'Learning how to die' is learning how to accomplish existence, of one's own existence, philosophically: it is as if to say that existence is that which is to be accomplished, in a manner that existing finitely one can appropriate one's own existence, make it one's ownmost reality and possibility, at its very limit, at the very abyss of dizzying height, even to the point of being shipwrecked and to the point of absolute impossibility of this very existence.

From Plato to Heidegger, with Hegel and even Nietzsche, philosophy has remained a certain finite thinking of appropriating finitude and death, as it were by a necessity which is difficult to bring to articulation, to disavow certain inconsolable mourning of an infinite finitude, of an endless dying, of a non-appropriable loss otherwise than being or negativity of nothing, otherwise than even nothingness which Heidegger tries to think more primordially than negativity of certain dialectical-speculative onto-theo-logy.[4] *Dasein* must appropriate his own death, which is in each singular case his proper: his nothingness, beyond the negativity of the Concept (Hegelian Concept of the concept, for example), belongs to his innermost being that is *his* as such as the very gift: Dasein is *attuned* to this 'nothingness in anxiety' as it were anticipating what is his utter impossibility to be 'to be,' insofar as Dasein is in each case of *existing* ex-sists ex-tatically *in its way to be.*[5]

That Dasein always exists ex-tatically *in its way to be*, that means, Dasein is this non-closure of ecstatic futurity, its possibility is always in any ecstatic temporality an anticipative impossibility of no-longer being able be its way to be. Is not even here finitude, as ex-tatic temporality of its way to be, insofar as it is anticipated—and Dasein anticipates it in its being-ahead of itself in each case—finitude remains the scandal of philosophy, philosophy's vain consolation, its vain attempts to remove the poisonous bite of death. Already in Plato's Socrates, this scandal is announced in the philosopher's attempt to come to terms with his own death by asking the mourned women to be driven away: with this disavowal of mourning—and also one must not forget that tragic poets do not have a place in the *Republic*—a certain metaphysical determination of politics is announced. Elsewhere in another place, I attempt to bring out the innermost connection of this metaphysical determination of politics, mourning, and finitude.

How does this dominant determination of politics, in its innermost relationship with finitude and death, inhabit secretly even in Heidegger's *Dasein*? To be able to appropriate one's own death, for each one dies his death: if that is to be resolute, to be decisive in stern decision to be authentic, which means not to tarry along in the state of fallenness, this implies to be resolute not to mourn one's own death, to refuse the impossibility that does not give the very possibility of being, to refuse to die without consolation and profit of meaning—not in the name of immortality of the soul nor in the name of the eternity of the Concept that happens eternally (which as Schelling ironically says of Hegel, happening that does not happen at all but happens only in thought)[6]—but in finitude, nay, as finite, out of its ecstatic groundlessness and nothingness. The consolation of death and refusal of mourning neither lie in the promise of immortality nor in the negativity of the Concept, but in existing itself as finite. With Heidegger the finitude of *Dasein* is its very consolation: such is the immanence of *Dasein* in the imminence of 'no more able to be,' though *Dasein* ex-sists ex-tatically insofar as it is its transcendence in each case, and there is its *care*, not is its concern and solicitude which it has for entities other than *Dasein* and entities which are other Daseins but with whom *Dasein* exists proximally in everyday inauthentic manner. To care for *Dasein* is to care for his own finitude in authentic manner, to exist in its ownmost possibility to die his own death: this means, care is care not to mourn for one's own death and not to mourn others' death, that means not to die others' death—

for anyway one does not die others' death—for to mourn others' death' and also one's, is to exist inauthentically in the falling state of Dasein, the inauthenticity that lies in refusing death of one's own, in refusing one's own, very own finitude, to refuse to accomplish one's own appropriate existence and appropriate death whose very possibility is its impossibility to be any more. To refuse what alone is the absolute possibility in its lone absolute impossibility, to disavow what is alone the possibility of accomplishing one's own death and existence is to be irresolute, to be indecisive, to succumb to the vacillating, ambiguous, inauthentic falling, and not to be stern in the face of the inconsolable mourning. 'To learn to die' is, whether in Plato or Heidegger, is to learn not to mourn: irresolute and indecisive beings, such as women are thought to be (in Platonic or rather in Socratic Metaphysics, for example), fragile and fainting, do not know enough of dying and therefore they also mourn too much; *the essential metaphysical determination of politics that is decisionist, resolute and stern in the face of finitude and mourning which intimates Platonic metaphysics, also intimates, inhabits, determines the innermost essence of the very Heideggerian destruction of that very metaphysics.* 'To learn to die' is to, what Hegel says of death, look death face to face and to be able to "tarry" with it: such is the metaphysics of death that in Hegel's case, that converts even non-being into being, is the very labour and accomplishment of this conversion.[7] Even here death remains the accomplishment, the resoluteness in the face of the negativity, to 'tarry with it' so that death does not take away anything without return of a profit: this sternness, this resolute philosophical heroism gives a certain tragic resonance to philosophical thinking, that finds speculative-dialectical articulation in Hegel. Is it not the same tragic heroism, despite Heidegger's *step back* from Hegelian onto-theo-logical metaphysics of *labor* and its *negativity,* of Subject and the vicissitudes of its dialectical *Aufhebung*, remains the intimation of Heidegger's being-towards-his-death, though this death would not be thought as Concept but that Dasein ex-tatically anticipates? 'To learn to die' as 'not to die an improper death, an inauthentic death'—in each case: Socrates,' Hegel's, Heidegger's—which is, not to mourn, for to mourn is improper to the proper, resolute, authentic death; or, to mourn is to mourn a death that is improper, inauthentic. If Socrates wanted the mourned women to be driven away, it is not only because mourning is excessive, which philosophical discourse of measurement and justice (insofar as justice measures and measurement is just) demands to sober up, but that mourning is really inappropriate and improper to the decorum that befits philosophical death. 'To philosophize is to learn how to die' is in each case, thus, is a question of conduct, which may not be prescriptive in some 'objective codes': there is a mode of dying that is proper and authentic and the other is not; there is a mode of dying that is appropriate because it appropriates death itself, there is a dying that is falling and inappropriate. There is also a language, a discourse appropriate to each mode of dying: resolute, *stubborn silence of the heroic-tragic man is the appropriate language (beyond language) of his in the face of the utter impossibility of his being whose very silence is his triumph in the face of his annihilation, the final laughter at the summit of existence resounding the dizzying height looking down to the yawning abyss.* To refuse to speak, this reticence in the face of his death: this speechlessness is the very proper to tragic-heroic man whose stubborn speechlessness alone is his triumph, that is, not to mourn and thus not to be taken away his death from himself, though he is taken away by death. This stubborn speechlessness, this resolute silence and decisive relation to one's own finitude: this metaphysics of the tragic intimates the innermost essence of Heidegger's tragic thinking of finitude. 'To learn how to die' is also to learn how to speak, tragically, that means, how to be silent and to be stubborn in that: this tragic-heroic determination of metaphysics intimates Dasein in the face of his ecstatic finitude; this is the very transport and ecstasy of tragic Dasein, his elevation beyond the everyday averageness of the inauthentic death of others, his sublimity in his very finitude, his final language at his own limit which is his impossibility to be. Does this not explain Heidegger's resolute, stubborn, enigmatic silence about his politics, about his great 'errancy'? It is his very politics that bestows a tragic resonance to the very innermost essence of his philosophy, which is not a question of merely accidentally joining a certain party for a certain accidental period of a lifetime: it also intimates the stubborn, tragic silence of a man who errs, essentially and greatly, out of his groundless freedom, and therefore unforgivably. Is silence only the speech that properly conveys the tragic ethos of a stubborn, resolute, heroic man who decisively, at the limit, responds to his own finitude that is absolutely his, his death, by defiantly refusing to speak, thereby even at his death, he defiantly affirms what is most properly his, his fate and character, for the tragic heroic being, his death must constitute at once his limit and at this limit, his very fate, his fulfilled destiny? Or there is another silence, otherwise than the defiant speechlessness of the tragic heroic man responding to his finitude resolutely, a silence otherwise than the tragic appropriation of one's own death at the limit, but rather a silence that marks the very limit of all appropriation, at the limit of language, and thereby attuned itself to the lament of a mourning? Such silence is not the pathos of a tragic heroic man of finitude, who faces alone his own impossibility and therefore alone redeems his only possibility, that is, to be impossible. To think such silence, as the lament of mourning, beyond the defiant appropriation of finitude, it is necessary to think silence and of language otherwise than the tragic heroic pathos of solitary man or of ecstatic Dasein's being-towards-his-death or the philosopher's learning to die. If language remains tied to death—as both Hegel and Heidegger, who understood death differently[8], think so, that is only so far as silence—not the silence of the tragic-heroic pathos of defiant Self but rather one that is intimated with lament of mournfulness—remains the limit of language itself, that makes of a dying inappropriable for us: it is this what marks the finitude of the finite beings, finitude of the man who speaks. At the limit of language silence intimates the lament of finitude, not as the work of death, thus beyond the dialectical-speculative-tragic appropriation of death, but as the sheer unworking of language, the infinite fatigue of language, its tears and tearing unrepaired within the language, let alone in the philosophical salvation in the Concept and hence that marks the limit of the power and pain of the negative.

Does one learn how to die this death? Does philosophizing enable one to die a death which is forever inappropriable, that marks the limit of all possibility and hence beyond the decision and indecision, beyond the fate and immortality? Who learns to die and from whom?

III

'To die,' for the tragic-heroic man, is to die silently. This defiance marks even the meta-ethical ethos of Rosenzweig's tragic man insofar as this man is not mere individual or personality but Self, his very *character*: his fate lies in his refusal to speak and thereby breaking all bridges not only between himself and other finite beings, but even with Gods and the World. Thus in Greek Attic tragedy, especially in the works of Aeschylus, Rosenzweig finds the purer expression of this fateful silence of meta-ethical man, as contrast to the non-tragic Asians (India and China).[9] The heroic ethos of the tragic man belongs properly to the meta-ethos: beyond the ethos of individuality and personality, the meta-ethical man' by defiance of his free will' elevates himself above his connection with his mere progeniture that links him with others and with the universality of genus. That is why the birth and death of the Self or of Character of the tragic man is not synonymous with the birth and death of individuals and personality; rather otherwise, the birth of the Self, this defiant Self of the tragic man is precisely the death of the individual and personality, death that assaults him first in disguise as *Eros* and than as *Thanatos* without disguise. The birth of the defiant Self, its only possibility to be lies in this most abysmal death that assaults him, at the very limit of his language and his being: from then on, this *daimon* silently accompanies him, as it accompanies Socrates, beyond the moral universal order of ethics shared by others; from then on his death alone is his "sovereign event,"[10] it alone constitutes his fate and therein he responds fatefully with his decisive, stern, resolute silence, in his refusing to speak to Gods and others and the World, in refusing to communicate with the universal moral order where there are only personalities. Yet this death, death of the absolutely solitary man, cut off from Gods and mortals alike to which the defiant Self of tragic man responds by refusing to speak, this death alone constitutes absolutely his Self as such, this silence alone constitutes his language as such which he responds fatefully, resolutely. Therefore silence alone is proper to the tragic hero of the meta-ethical man: that marks his sublimity and elevation, his fate and singularity, his very *'selfication.'* Thus Rosenzweig says,

> For that is the criterion of the self, the seal, the seal of its greatness as well as the stigma of its weakness: it keeps silent. The tragic hero has only one language which completely corresponds to him: precisely keeping silent. It has thus from the beginning. The tragedy casts itself in the artistic form of drama just in order to be able to represent speechlessness...by keeping silent 'the hero breaks down the bridges which connect him with God and the world, and elevates himself out of the fields of personality' delimiting itself and individualizing itself from others in speech, into the icy solitude of self.[11] And, the hero as such as to succumb only because his demise entitles him to the supreme "heroization," to wit, the most closed-off "selfication" of his self. He yearns for this solitude of demise' because there is no greater solitude than this. Accordingly the hero does not actually die after all. Death only cuts him off, as it were, from the temporal features of individuality. Character transmitted into heroic self is immortal. For him, eternity of just good enough to echo his silence.[12]

This heroic, defiant, tragic pathos, this resolute refusal to speak even unto death that entitles one's own death to be one's own, this jargon of elevation of authenticity, of sublimity of heroic sacrifice, this selfication in its very demise, this stubborn holding onto one's death of the solitary sky and earth: this pathos marks the very ethos of a certain dominant metaphysics of death. Death at the end must be able to give each one—to the philosopher learning to die, to Dasein in his being-towards-his-death, to the historical becoming of Spirit in its negativity, to the tragic, meta-ethic man of silence—his own death, that death must be one's own, that death must at the end be one's own possibility of immortality and or his authentic being, death that would be appropriate and appropriable, a capability and possibility, death that would at the end give one his very Self or being in relation to which the stubborn silence refusing to share his elevation and solitude with others would be maintained: this stern language has remained the dominant metaphysics of death.[13] And this metaphysics of death, in various forms and shapes, determines itself on a certain dominant thinking of tragedy and tragic: the questions of sacrifice and community, language and being, temporality and finitude—all these questions that are at stake here, are already determined on the basis of this tragic heroic ethos, ethos that intimate the Greek tragic heroes to the philosophical heroism of 'learning to die.'

IV

When for a finite being his own existence becomes for the first time the question of his fate? When he for the first time asks 'who am 'I'? These two questions have an innermost connection in that the question of fate is inwardly bound up with the question of Self, or character: so one asks, when for the finite being, his Self becomes, that alone, the sovereign fate, "the sovereign event" of his existence? When a finite being comes to face with the most sovereign necessity, the most ineluctable destiny that his Self must become his fate, and that alone, and that his fate lies in that he must be *Self*? As if the very notion of 'fate' is bound up, in an ineluctable manner, with the 'selfication' of self; where, then, this necessity arise, the necessity of 'selfhood' for the finite being, for the necessity of 'self-hood' seems meaningful only for finite being, insofar as one is finite? Only for the finite being the necessity seems to arise for 'selfhood,' for 'selfication' and his 'selfication' as his fate, his destiny, his necessity; his fate, his Self is, thus, bound up with his finitude, the utter groundlessness of his being, the abyss of his nothingness.

Therefore the question of fate and character, the selfhood of the Self lies in this: when one confronts death, when one looks into the abyss, the utter impossibility of his Self, the groundlessness of his being or existing and then and there the necessity arises, in the face of death that has become one's "sovereign event", to constitute oneself to be the necessity, the stern fate and resolute Self; the most inescapable demand, then, arises to convert even the nothingness of one's abysmal existence into the most defiant Self and resolute character. Therefore only someone who has character is said to have fate or to be fateful; in other words, only someone who is Self has his fate; it is the fate of the one who has seen death in face and, as Hegel says, stays "tarrying with it"[14] and not only that, he converts his groundlessness into the very ground of his self, into the very condition and possibility of his being. The birth of Self, the condition of "Selfhood" of Self, thus, lies when the abyss of death reveals itself and the finite human being looks with unspeakable horror at his utter impossibility: his every comfort in the world, his faith in the solidity and subsistence of existence, his trust in the arrangement of human destiny and its historicity is at once shattered and lost. This impossible experience of death makes the finite being attuned to a certain fundamental attunement of melancholia, a certain impossibility of dying as if one is already always dead and that his death has already been taken away from him. This sadness oppresses, Hegel says, even the animals: so the animal or the bird of prey does not even wait looking at his victim; he jumps into it and annihilates it.[15] This sadness separates him, thenceforth, from the world in which he exists with others as individual and also cuts him off from God: from then on silently he carries his own death, or rather his death carries him in a sovereign manner, alone in absolute solitude, while he is still with others, speaks to them in the manner everyone speaks, suffers similar predicaments and pain, strives for same things like others and entertains himself with the same pleasures. Yet something, that terrible thing that happened to him in his absolute solitude, which he henceforth is carried silently like a silent companion, this constitutes his absolute secret: he says everything thenceforth to everyone, yet the essential thing, the only sovereign thing for him, that alone remains unspoken; this secret will then separate him from everyone and everything else in the world and make him, as separate and different from others, his 'Self,' his distinct fate, his solitary sovereign destiny. Something remains incommunicable and uncommunicated thenceforth: this secret is his self, and since this is his "sovereign event", that must be for him his 'fate,' to which he can only respond fatefully. From that fateful moment onwards, when his Self is born, precisely when he died, he responds to everything in the world which arise and pass away in a mortal manner, in a fateful manner: as if in a certain manner he is always already dead, as if death is not like what it is for ordinary conception, namely, a datable event at the end of life, but rather for him at any moment of his existing he is already always dead as possible; as if then onwards the "empirical", datable event no longer matters any more as final annihilation.

He responds to his death, thenceforth, no more like "everyday","inauthentic manner"' for everyday Dasein does not have fate or destiny (we can understand here why for a tragic philosopher like Heidegger "destiny" is such a dear word), he responds fatefully to his ecstatic destiny, beyond average levelling of "datable" death, for "datable" death (which is investigated by regional ontologies, and thus in a manner of entities *Vorhandenheit)* is precisely for Heidegger non-fateful, inauthentic death. Or like Hegel, he looks at life with an empty gaze of the philosopher: existence fleets by in front of it, but his gaze does not waver, for any wavering anyway does not bring anything new. Or he makes his own self the defiant response to his own death, making it the occasion for the very possibility of his self, albeit a vain triumph and impossible assertion, for it takes away from him his very possibility. This is the response of the tragic man of meta-ethic, the heroic ethos of defiance: his non-communication and silence, his secret and solitude, his selfhood and his fate, his character and his death. There seems something like tragic about the philosopher's empty gaze and something philosophical about the tragic defiance: they are responses to the abyss of being, the groundlessness of existence, the finitude of all finite beings; they are responses to death which haunts the philosophers and tragic hero alike and this response in turn constitutes the very dominant destiny of Western metaphysics. From the tragic, heroic, defiant response to nothingness and to death, there arises the tragic, heroic, defiant metaphysics. A tragic, heroic, defiant learning to die.

V

Can one die one's own death? Can one speak one's own speech, one's own language? Franz Rosenzweig's *The Star of Redemption* begins with the articulation of the innermost connection of philosophical death and philosophical language. If in the innermost manner, philosophical death is tied to the philosophical language that seeks to restore what is lost as *existence* in its immediate, sensuous finiteness, as if learning to die one's own death, one also learns to speak one's own language, no longer merely as the finite Self, but as what Rosenzweig says, "the Cognition of the All"; it is philosophy's vain attempt to retrieve, to recuperate, to resurrect—not the decaying as decaying, but as the transfigured presence—in language of what the earth can not claim, what is rescued from the unconscious elements of the earth.[16] Thus in his *Lectures on the Philosophy of Religion*, Hegel speaks of the nullity of a death that is nothing but already implicitly negative, and also nullity of mourning and fear that the man of the religion of nature bewails at this null, vain finitude:

> The natural, simple self-emancipation of the finite from its finiteness is death. This is the renunciation of the finite and here what the natural life is itself implicitly is made explicit really and actually. The sensuous life of what is individual or particular has its end in death. Particular experiences or sensations as particular are transient; one supplants the other, one impulse or other drives away the another ... In death the finite is shown to be annulled and absorbed. But death is only abstract negation of what is implicitly negative; it is itself a nullity, it is revealed a nullity. But explicit nullity is at the same time nullity which has been done away with, and is the return to the positive. Here cessation, liberated from finiteness, comes in. Death does not present itself to consciousness as this emancipation from finiteness, but this higher view of death is found in thought, and indeed even in popular conceptions, insofar as thought is active in them.[17]

What of the death philosophy attempts to think then, if not the death that has lost its poisonous sting, in the philosophical language in which the mortal cry of the fear of death is not heard, where the abyss of the grave is not revealed? Finally, it seems that philosophy is neither capable of consoling us from death, death with its sting, nor is it capable of language; philosophy has remained thus without death and without language, or rather it thinks of a death which nobody dies, and speaks a language which nobody speaks; by thinking death only as negative, as "nought" of thinking itself, and by subordinating language to thinking, philosophy remains without language and a vain attempt to take from us the fear of death. By depriving the singular from the universal, philosophy which is "cognition of the All" vainly attempts to console us by presenting a death made harmless by depriving its poison, for only singular dies, and only the singular speaks, as if by a necessity within philosophical discourse, each time the demand of thinking death arises so as to be profited from it, the demand not to drink its poison, demand not to die a poisonous death necessarily announces itself in advance, by a necessity to avert its gaze not to look death face to face, not to look directly at the groundless abyss of its own condition, only as "not-not" but not "it is". Thus Rosenzweig says,

> For indeed, an All would not die and nothing would die in the All. Only the singular can die and everything mortal is solitary. Philosophy has to rid the world of what is singular, and this un-doing of the Aught is also the reason why it has to be idealistic. For idealism, with its denial of everything that distinguishes the singular from the All, is the tool of the philosopher's trade. With it, philosophy continues to work over the recalcitrant material until the latter finally offers no more resistance to the smoke screen of the one-and-all concept. If once all were woven into this mist, death would indeed be swallowed up, if not into the eternal triumph, at least into the one and universal night of the Nought. And it is the ultimate conclusion of this doctrine that death is—Nought.[18]

Death is "nought": if to philosophize is learn that death is "nought", the nullity of mourning for a death that is nullity itself, this nullity itself remains inconsolable for the singular and solitary, for the one who is mortal and abandoned. Hence Socrates' vain attempts to console the mourned women at his death: between Socrates' relation to his own death and the women's relation to Socrates' death, there remained unaddressed the place of mourning, this caesura in the philosophical discourse, caesura that marks the limit of this philosophical lesson of learning how to die.

VI

"Die at the right time": this is also the teaching of Zarathustra.[19] Death must not be a creeping thief but the consummation and squandering of the victorious soul. Is not the most abysmal thought of eternal return, the abysmal thought of the death of God is no other than the thought of dying itself? Then "to die" is essentially a task, the most abysmal task which only the squandering, great soul can accomplish, and which marks the very consummation of his tragic adventure: it is the task of the one who throws the golden ball and consummates his existence like the timely fruit, it is the task of the one who transforms himself from camel in the desert to the lion and then to the child, who walks over the bridge of man—for "man is the bridge and not his own end"[20]—so that this squandering, autumnal hero is also the rope walker, rope that hangs over the abyss of time. Death must not be the objection of him who walks over his own abyss but the very consummation of his tragic existence, for in dying rightly he also overcomes the revenge of time with a tragic laughter: such is the meaning of the eternal return as the thought of death, for the eternal return redeems time, time that comes creeping and closes itself, arises and falls itself in generating and passing, the labour of the historical, homogeneous, empty time. By freeing oneself from the labour of the empty, historical, homogeneous time—time that comes creeping like the thief—is to free oneself for death that consummates the great squandering, victorious soul that while consummating, also redeems it: the thought of the eternal return, as the thought of death, is thus the thought of the redemption of historical, homogeneous, empty time. Yet this almost messianic sounding thought of eternal return—the contemporary philosophers like Gérard Bensussan[21] brings to articulation the innermost affinity, if not identity, of the thought of eternal return with the thought of the messianic—is also intimated by the tragic resonance of the heroic ethos, the very ethos that Nietzsche's thought of eternal return otherwise puts into question, the ethos of sacrifice on the basis of which from Socrates' death to Zarathustra's thought of death the very understanding of community and language is determined, the ethos on the basis of which certain metaphysics of sovereignty and Subject is determined, the ethos for which death has remained a 'possibility' and mastery of a 'sovereign event'. Nay, it is the very source of sovereignty itself, the sovereignty of death. I attempt to articulate the innermost connection of this tragic heroic ethos of sacrifice, thought in relation to a certain determination of death and work, of certain determination time and history with what came to thought of the questions of community and language, thus the very thought of politics and the political.

VII

'Learning to die' at the right time? Is it not that death is always untimely, either too late or too early for one to die and hence never to be learnt, dying that began already in a beginningless time, time that is lost never to be recuperated, it already falls outside of all positing and op-positing in the very positing and time that remains, never to be anticipated but only hoped time: does this time, time that is lapsed in the un-memorial, time that intimates us in our deepest melancholy and also the time that remains for us to hope, does this time arrive at the right time, at the appropriate and appropriable time, at a possible and anticipatable and recuperable time? Can this time be thought on the basis of death, of tragic death that has learnt to die at the right time, to die heroically that befits a resolute Dasein, or Defiant Meta-ethical tragic man, or a heroic philosopher, or the one who throws the golden ball, who affirms chance and thus redeems the empty time? Is it not that to mourn for the lapse of time, not the once present time of accomplishment and accomplishing time of presence, but the already always untimely falling away of time and to hope a time that remains, not the anticipatable time for consummating heroic accomplishment in death, but non-anticipatable hoped time that is coming—is not such time otherwise than tragic time of heroic fulfilment, and must be thought otherwise than such an ethos and pathos of the tragic determination of death and finitude? Is not such time of mourning otherwise than, more primordial than the anticipatable time of anxiety over Dasein' own imminent death, for mourning is more primordially attuned to finitude than anxiety as the fundamental attunement of finitude? Would not the time of hope, lengthened to infinity, exceeding the closure of dialectical-speculative determination of presence and beyond the metaphysics of speculative historical time, be the time of redemption, or time that redeems time itself, which cannot be thought either as the sublated time of Concept without language or as the tragic time of speechlessness? How can such time, untimely time, time outside time be thought, time that intimates our finitude in the attunements of melancholy and hope, time of un-memorial, never-present-never-accomplished lost time and time of hope for the coming, that inexhaustible time of the remains? As if it were time itself must be released from time, not in the name of the eternity of the Concept, nor in the tragically fulfilled time for the heroic, nor the laborious time of the negativity, nor the ex-tatic finitude of 'possibility of the impossibility' of Dasein, but time that is finite each time, that is limited time, singular and as this trans-immanence, releases time from its own closure, as that which falls outside of itself in its very arriving, so that what arrives in the very arriving diverts as what is never posited as such in any present time and also so that time remains to arrive, since what has arrived as accomplished time of present has not accomplished all time, has remained unfulfilled and unaccomplished' so that a time remains to come, which is very arrival itself that would not be exhausted. What has remained to come is an "advent" which is at once the very thought of releasement of time and finitude: this thought of advent and releasement is attuned to our fundamental attunement of melancholy and hope, melancholy for the un-memorial time of lapsed time and hope for the time for arriving. As such melancholy and hope are the very fundamental attunements of finitude, the attunements that mark the finitude of our finite existence: as finite beings, whose condition is never appropriable, that cannot own one's own ground, we are attuned to our finitude in melancholy and hope. We are melancholic and hopeful insofar as we are finite, that finitude is not an accidental property of our existence. Our existence is this very gift of finitude. If humans speak, it is not because man is capable of death, not because death is a possibility for man, but rather speech or language is the very gift of finitude. This gift is attuned to us and intimates us, at the very limit of language, in the lament of silence, in our mourning and melancholy, in our hope for the time to come and in the redemption of coming: they mark the very limit of our power of appropriation, the power and pain of the negative. And we must be grateful and thankful for this gift, the finite gift of language. To think finitude anew demands that the closure of this dominant edifice of metaphysics is to be disclosed and to open it to the advent of releasement. What is meant hereby 'the advent of releasement' shall only be clear when the closure of the dominant metaphysics is opened to this advent. In taking the problematic of time and finitude as the fundamental issue, I attempt to think that the advent of releasement as an essentially fundamental ethico-political exigency of our time: a finite politics, or ethics of finitude insofar as finitude is no longer to be seen as dialectical-speculative other of infinite concept, but non-negative finitude as releasement' the releasement of the advent.[23] Reading Schelling, Heidegger, and Rosenzweig, this advent of releasement—as essentially finite, and beyond the dialectical-speculative determination of time—is elaborated as essentially an ethico-political task of remembrance and arriving, in its innermost connection with melancholy and hope, the fundamental attunements of finite existence. The intimation of mournfulness in language resonates, I argue, an intimate connection between the very receiving and giving of the gift and a certain melancholy.[24] Yet there is also something else: there is an intimation of hope in language, an intimate connection between the very receiving and giving of the gift and a certain hope for the coming, a hope for redemption in the coming, a hope for what remains, as if in the very gift of language, we are not only intimated with a certain mournfulness, but in hope we open ourselves to the very time that remains: in speaking and in language, we do not become capable of death, but as already finite, beyond our capacity and possibility, at the limit of our appropriation, we are given over to melancholy and hope.

What is this relationship between time and language, between time and our fundamental attunements of finitude, namely, melancholy and hope, time otherwise than either tragic time or the historical time of presence or ex-tatic time of a finite Dasein? What is the relationship between dying and language, of a dying that intimates, inhabits our language with an intimation of mourning that pushes language itself to its limit, and marks the finitude and limit of our appropriation in a manner that the philosophical discourse is exposed to its own abyss which it cannot recuperate and console, as if mourning inhabits and tears asunder the philosophical discourse itself, from within itself? And finally what is the relationship between language and community, community and time, and community and death, if language and death and time be thought otherwise than on the modality of tragic sacrifice or otherwise than the metaphysics of historical subject, otherwise than the closure of dialectical-speculative appropriation?

Who learns how to die? The one who remains? Or the one who is no longer? From whom does one learn to die? The one who remains? Or the one who is no longer?

NOTES

1. "Phaedo," in *The Trial and Execution of Socrates*, trans. by Peter George (London: The Folio Society, MCMLXXII, 1972), p. 103.
2. F.W.J. von Schelling, *Philosophical Investigation into the Nature of Human Freedom,* trans. James Gutmann (La Salle, Illinois: Open Court,1992).
3. Martin Heidegger, *Schelling's Treatise on the Essence of Human Freedom,* trans. by Joan Stambaugh (Athens: Ohio University Press,1985), pp. 6-7.
4. Martin Heidegger, "What is Metaphysics?" in *Pathmarks*, ed. by William McNeill (Cambridge: Cambridge University Press, 1998), pp. 82-96.
5. Martin Heidegger, *Being and Time,* trans. by John Macquarrie and Edward Robinson (New York: Harper & Row, 1962), pp. 274-311.
6. F.W.J. von Schelling, *On the History of Modern Philosophy,* trans. by Andrew Bowie (Cambridge: Cambridge University Press, 1994), pp. 134-160.
7. G.W.F. Hegel, *Phenomenology of Spirit,* trans. by A.V. Miller (Delhi: Motilal Benarasidass, 1998), p. 19.

8. Thus Heidegger, in his *What is Metaphysics?*, attempts to think of nothing in a more originary manner than Hegelian negativity, the later constitutive of a speculative logic: "the nothing is the origin of negation, not vice versa. If the power of the intellect in the field of inquiry into the nothing and into being is thus shattered' then the destiny of the reign of "logic" in philosophy is thereby decided. The idea of "logic" itself disintegrates into turbulence of a more originary questioning." Heidegger, *Pathmarks*, p. 92.
9. I am profited from a discussion with Gèrard Bensussan who rightly pointed out to me that for Rosenzweig the silent defiance of the mythic-tragic hero is not the end or finality 'but constitutes only the beginning' the point of departure towards what demands going beyond the tragic-mythic world of the Greek individuality. Having agreed with him, I am interested to see that the textual logic that governs Rosenzweig's *The Star of Redemption* precisely enables Rosenzweig to contrast the Tragic-mythic world of Greek individuality with the un-mythic Asians (Indian and Chinese) with the clear privilege given to the tragic world of Greek individuality. Thus towards the end of *The Star of Redemption* not only are Indian and Chinese religions left behind as un-mythic, but even Islam as a world religion is portrayed in a not so favourable light. Christianity and Jewish religions alone have remained destinal religions, surpassing the un-mythic Asian and the Islamic religion. Undoubtedly a Hegelian historical systematic still governs Rosenzweig's textual logic, which otherwise is a polemic against Hegelian Idealist philosophy.
10. Franz Rosenzweig, *The Star of Redemption,* trans. by William W. Hallo (London: Routledge and Kegan Paul, 1971), pp. 76-77.
11. Ibid., p. 77.
12. Ibid. pp. 78-79.
13. If I have here pointed out that each of these thinkers—Heidegger, Rosenzweig's mythic hero and Nietzsche—has a certain thinking or valorisation of a tragic heroic death in its intimate connection with language, this is not to level off, or to put into the same basket Heidegger's tragic acceptance of Nazi Ideology with Rosenzweig's messianic affirmation. These two have different levels of discourse; or rather they have two different discursive histories. What I am attempting here is only to point out that death is in *each* case with these thinkers, that means *differently* and *singularly*, is understood as 'possibility': this 'possibility' has a certain discursive metaphysical history, the articulation of which is a different thing than their political allegiance. Thus it

ought not to be concluded that because both Heidegger's Dasein and Rosenzweig's mythic-heroic man assert resolutely a tragic death—that thereby one's tragic assertion of Nazi Ideology is immediately juxtaposed, or levelled off with the other's messianic affirmation of a time beyond violence.

14. G.W.F. Hegel, *Phenomenology of Spirit* (1988), p. 19.
15. G.W.F. Hegel, *Phenomenology of Spirit,* trans. by A.V. Miller (Oxford: Clarendon Press, 1979), p. 65.
16. See Hegel, *Phenomenology of the Spirit.*
17. G.W.F. Hegel, *Lectures on the Philosophy of Religion*, Vol. I, trans. by E.B. Speirs (London: Routledge and Kegan Paul, 1962), p. 182.
18. Rosenzweig, *The Star of Redemption*, p. 4.
19. Friedrich Nietzsche, *Thus Spoke Zarathustra*, trans. by Walter Kaufmann (New York: Modern Library,1995), pp. 71-73.
20. See Gérard Bensussan, "Has Zarathustra Any Hope?," in *Nietzsche: Philologist, Philosopher and Cultural Critic*, ed. by Franson Manjali (New Delhi: Allied Publishers, 2006), pp. 43-50
21. Gérard Bensussan, *Le Temps Messianque: Temps Historique et Temps Vècu* (Paris: Vrin, 2001).

4

Walter Benjamin's Messianic Conception of History

I

In his *Theologico-Political Fragment*, Walter Benjamin writes,

> Only the messiah himself consummates all history, in the sense that he alone redeems, completes, creates its relation to the Messianic. For this reason, nothing historical can relate itself on its own account to anything Messianic. Therefore the Kingdom of God is not the *telos* of the historical dynamic; it cannot be set as a goal. From the standpoint of history it is not the goal but the end. Therefore the order of the profane cannot be built up on the idea of the Divine Kingdom and therefore theocracy has no political but only a religious meaning.

And,

> The profane, therefore, although not itself a category of this Kingdom, is a decisive category of its quietest approach. For in happiness all that is earthly seeks its downfall, and only in good fortune is its downfall destined to find it. Whereas, admittedly, the immediate Messianic intensity of the heart, of the inner man in isolation, passes through misfortune, as suffering. To the spiritual *restitutio in integrum*, which introduces immortality, corresponds a worldly restitution that leads to the eternity of downfall, and the rhythm of this eternally transient worldly existence, transient in its totality, the rhythm of messianic nature, is happiness. For nature is Messianic by reason of its eternal and total passing away.
>
> To strive after such passing, even for those stages of man that are nature, is the task of world politics, whose method must be called nihilism.[1]

This fragment, in a cryptic manner, gives us the Benjaminian idea of world-nihilist politics. There is no such thing called "messianic politics", if the concept of the political can be understood as legitimization of the sovereignty of the worldly power in the profane order. In fact, the notion of messianicity, understood in the old theocratic sense, that means, in its eschatological intensity, can only have religious significance that bases itself upon the non-contemporeinty or non-analogy of the divine and the profane order. This means, messianicity, understood in its relation to the historical reason, can only be thought as de-legitimization of all attempts to found sovereignty on the basis of the analogy to the divine fulfilment. In relation to the earthly sovereignty in the profane order, the messianic arrival does not serve itself as foundation of new law through suspension of the old. It rather welcomes the total passing away of what must pass away, the complete downfall of the entire order of transiency. It is in this sense only can one say that messianism is suspension of law in any radical sense. It is not the un-founding of one earthly order in order to found another with equal or even more powerful act of sovereignty but suspension of the mythic order in *toto*. As such the divine violence—which is the messianic violence without violence (without the two fold law-preserving and law-destroying violence)—has no political meaning but only a religious one. Between the divine violence—which has only religious sense —and the mythic violence, there is an abyss of non-foundation, of a difference that defers and differs any attempts at legitimization of the worldly sovereignties on a theological foundation.

II

Thus, messianism is a state of exception. It is a state of exception without law: with this insistence on the irreducibility of justice to law that Benjamin radically departs from Carl Schmitt. The state of exception of the messianic arrival refuses to level itself off to the state of exception that founds law by suspending law. With this, Benjamin overturns the Schmittean concept of the juridico-political. In the VIII thesis of his *Theses on the Philosophy of History*, Walter Benjamin criticizes Schmitt without naming him:

> The tradition of the oppressed teaches us that the "state of emergency" in which we live is not the exception but the rule. We must attain to a conception of history that accords with this insight. Then we will clearly see that it is our task to bring about a real state of emergency, and this will improve our position in the struggle against fascism.[2]

One can see here that the political theology which messianism in its eschatological intensity attains is not to be confused with the concept of political theology of Carl Schmitt.[3] Thus the concept of the political as that which is supposed to have been secularization of the theological[4] is seen to be radically heterogeneous to the messianic insistence on the irreducibility of justice to law. The world-nihilism of messianism, in contrast to the theological structure of the political sovereignties, is an exception without sovereignty. This can be seen even in the period of Benjamin's brief fascination with "the historical materialism" of Marx, a term which nowhere appears in Karl Marx's works. What is important for Benjamin here is not so much the classless society as the *telos* of a determinate historical movement, auto-engendering (therefore mythic), whose momentum is infinitely and irresistibly nourished by the energy of progress. It is rather the revolutionary politics of the world-nihilism, for the ideology of the progress of the determinate historical time is already shown to be nothing but an idea suitable to the victors. In the following words, taken from *Paralipomena to the Concept of History*, Benjamin attempts to bind together the thought of the messianic, on the one hand, and on the other, the revolutionary politics of Karl Marx's "historical materialism". Obviously, this bringing together of a world-nihilist messianic idea which distinguishes *telos* from the end with a dialectical thinking still informed by the historical time of progress is not without problem. It appears as if the messianic distinction of the end from *telos* does not go too well with the idea of dialectical history that tacitly presupposes an idea of time as auto-engendering, irresistibly moved by progress. And it appears as if the messianic-eschatological idea of catastrophe cannot be dialectically conceived. How to read the following lines:

The structure of Marx's basic idea is as follows: Through a series of class struggles, humanity attains to a classless society in the course of historical development. =But classless society is not to be conceived as the endpoint of historical development.= From this erroneous conception Marx's epigones have derived (among other things) the notion of the "revolutionary situation", which, as we know, has always refused to arrive. = A genuinely messianic face must be restored to the concept of classless society and to be sure, in the interest of furthering the revolutionary politics of the proletariat itself.

What does it mean to "restore messianic face to the concept of the classless society"? Didn't Marx's epigones[5] see that the most revolutionary element of Marx's thinking is not the moment of goal that is reached by historical progress by determinate and irresistible force of the negative but its other element which is obfuscated behind the determinate order of a historical reason? That other element is the eschatological element in Marxist thinking that de-legitimizes all acts of founding sovereignty in the profane order, the element which is the truly state of exception. But this eschatological arrival, so argues Benjamin here as elsewhere, cannot be set as the goal lying ahead of itself at the end of a homogeneous empty process, but that can appear at each and every moment, summoning up the infinite distance into nearness, and nearness into distance. "For the revolutionary thinker, the peculiar revolutionary chance offered by every historical moment gets its warrant from the political situation", writes Benjamin in Paralipomena[6]. In the discourse of Marx's epigone, this "each" and "every" moment—*Jetzeit* or Now Time—is reduced to a determinate moment of a determinate movement which is always receding to an indefinite horizon of non-arrival. As a result, the truly revolutionary politics of historical materialism transforms itself into what it is not supposed to be: it forgets the idea of the true state of exception and thus turns either into reactionary or conservative form of politics. The historical time becomes for it a movement of "homogeneous, empty time".[7]

III

It is important for us to recognize the fundamental distinction that Benjamin makes between the profane order of historical reason from the messianic intensity of suffering. It is on this basis of this distinction alone can one distinguish the true state of exception from those "states of emergency" that threaten to become rule. The true state of exception is the moment of consummation of history. This is the eschatological version of Benjamin's messianism. But this is not the only version of messianism to be found in Benjamin. In his other essays, like *Language as Such and Language of Man*, and *The Task of the Translator*, and also in his *Origin of German Tragic Drama*, Benjamin calls forth the other version of messianism that is connected with the restoration and restitution of the immemorially paradisiacal past that never came to pass by.[8] Such paradisiacal, Adamic condition must be renewed in philosophical contemplation, in translation and in our poetic language of naming without violence. In the eschatological version of Benjamin's revolutionary politics, Messiah alone can consummate history. This means historical reason can not attain, by means of its immanent force of progressive movement, its consummation. In his very early text of student days called *Trauerspiel and Tragedy*, Benjamin distinguishes the idea of messianic time from both tragic time and teleologically determined empirical-historical time.[9] While tragic time is the individually fulfilled time, and mechanical-historical time is the historically unfulfilled time, messianic time alone is historically fulfilled time. In this text Benjamin refers the messianic end of history as redemption which, as such, cannot be the goal or even an infinite task of history. The messianic idea of redemption for Benjamin in this early text is closely connected with happiness that, like a password, secretly passes through history, linking the immemorial past of a paradisiacal condition to the present that is endowed with the "weak Messianic power".[10]

IV

Whether Benjamin presents us the eschatological or the restitution-version of messianism, it is important for us to consider Benjamin's insistence on the irreducibility of the messianic end to the goal of historical reason, whether that historical reason assumes the form of Schmittean political theology or in Marx's various epigones. Despite their being so irreducibly different from each other in almost all respects, all these tendencies have one thing in common: they give themselves the task of legitimization of various forms of sovereignty in the profane order, while truly messianic intensity should be entirely otherwise, which is that of de-legitimization of all and every form of sovereignty in the profane order. Only a messianic intensity of time, in its utter fulfilment, can consummate history. That intensity of time which Benjamin calls *Now time* can be fulfilled by humans only in a weak messianic manner in the intensity of moment that suddenly advents in the very midst of indeterminate present, for it represents both transiency of eternity and eternity of transiency. This makes all acts of foundation of law and sovereignty in the profane order irreducibly finite and discontinuous, for consummation of history is at once negation of the order of historical time and the beginning of new calendar time. Here Benjamin uses a word to refer to such moment which has long inter-textual and inter-discursive context: that of St Augustine, Kierkegaard, Schelling, Rosenzweig and Heidegger among many others. The word is *Augenblick:* it is not an instant of time, as one instant among many instants that can be arranged quantitatively and additively in a homogeneous scale of homogeneity time; it is rather an arrest of time precisely at its fulfilment. *Augenblick* is the moment of fulfilment of all past potentiality, past that becomes citable in all its moments, the moment that explodes the continuum of history like "the prose which bursts the fetters of script". It is the moment when "dialectic stands still" in its eternal transiency and the human language turns into the sobriety of prose. It is not the prose which Hegel dreams, the painted prose of grey, which remembers what the images of the past the Spirit has passed through. It is rather the moment of another recollection which reads what is never written.

V

This problem is fundamental to thinkers who lived around the same time, that is, early part of the last century, thinkers like Franz Rosenzweig, Walter Benjamin, Ernst Bloch, Gershom Scholem and the young Jacob Taubes. This makes all these Jewish thinkers a kind of family resemblances. The problem is the messianic task that these diverse thinkers give themselves: de-legitimization of any institutions of earthly sovereignty of "man over man" in the profane, historical order. Against such institutions and against such appeal of earthly sovereignty to the divine foundation on the basis of analogy, they evoke the notion of messianic consummation or messianic inauguration of history. The idea of theocracy as that which can not be utilized as political concept but at best be seen to belong to the religious domain: this idea is founded upon a fundamental distinction between religion and politics. One can trace this idea in St Paul and as well as in Jewish Gnostics, in St Augustine as in various eschatological tendencies in early Christianity. This distinction is the distinction between worldly and spiritual, the pursuit of happiness in the historical time and the intensity of messianic travail. This is because the messianic conception wants to make heard an absolute demand which is so unconditional that it refuses to recognize itself in any historical, relative realization of it in the profane, historical order. Along with it, there is the profound awareness of the danger when the messianic-eschatological claim of redemption is immediately transformed into world-historical politics on the stage of history, a danger not only Benjamin but also Franz Rosenzweig in an epic manner elaborates in his *Star of Redemption.* The following are the words of Jacob Taubes, raising with and against his teacher Gershom Scholem, from a beautiful essay called "The Price of Messianism":

> If the messianic idea in Judaism is not interiorized, it can turn "the landscape of redemption" into a blazing apocalypse. If one is to enter irrevocably into history, it is imperative to beware of the illusion that redemption happens on the stage of history. For every attempt to bring about redemption on the level of history without a transfiguration of the messianic idea leads straight into abyss.[11]

This is the warning against all sorts of totalitarian politics. This is also the reason of Taubes' ever recurrent critique of Carl Schmitt, a critique that operates in Walter Benjamin's texts as well but in his usual aphoristic, cryptic, concentrated manner. Here is Taubes again,

> You see what I want from Schmitt—I want to show him that the separation of powers between worldly and spiritual is *absolutely necessary*. This boundary, if it is not drawn, we will lose our occidental breath. This is what I wanted to impress upon him against his totalitarian concept.[12]

Now, I hope, we can read again these lines of Benjamin with which I began: "Therefore the order of the profane cannot be built on the idea of the Divine Kingdom, and therefore theocracy has no political, but only a religious meaning. To have repudiated with utmost vehemence the political significance of theocracy is the cardinal merit of Bloch's *Spirit of Utopia*."[13]

The modern historical reason attempts to erase this distinction in a new ground. For Hegel, history is essentially a theodicy. This secularization of the theological, or rather founding embodiment of the divine in the earthly sovereignty, the messianic idea of redemption is immediately transformed into a *telos* of an immanent historical reason. All the forms of historical reason that Benjamin denounces in *Theses on the Philosophy of History* have arisen from this transformation, whether it is universal history of progress, positivism of Neo-Kantianism, the political programmes of the Social Democratic Party, the empathy of the dominant historical narrative of transmission with the victors that refuses to look back at the unredeemed suffering of the past in the name of the facile idea of progress coming in future that is forever unrealized and unrealizable.

NOTES

1. "The Theologico-Political Fragment" in *Reflections*, edited by Peter Demetz (New York: Schocken Press, 1986), pp. 312-313.
2. "Theses on the Philosophy of History" in *Illuminations*, edited by Hannah Arendt, trans. Harry Zohn (New York: Schocken, 1985), p. 257.

3. See Carl Schmitt's, *Political Theology,* trans., George Schwab (Chicago: University of Chicago Press, 2005); *Political Theology II,* trans. Michael Hoelzl and Graham Ward (Cambridge: Polity Press, 2008).
4. Thus Schmitt could write in *Political Theology,* "all significant concepts of the modern theory of the state are secularized theological concepts not only because of their historical development—in which they were transferred from theology to the theory of the state, whereby, for example, the omnipotent God became the omnipotent lawgiver—but also because of their systematic structure, the recognition of which is necessary for a sociological consideration of these concepts. The exception in jurisprudence is analogous to the miracle in theology. Only by being aware of this analogy can we appreciate the manner in which the philosophical ideas of the state developed in the last centuries"(p. 36).
5. In *Theses on the Philosophy of History,* Benjamin not only cites Social Democrats but progressivism of all sorts: this includes not only the positivistic conception of historical reason, but also the Kantian regulative idea of an "infinite task".
6. Walter Benjamin, "Paralipomena to the Concept of History" *in Selected Writings, 1938-40,* Vol. 4 (The Belknap Press, 2006), pp. 401-411.
7. Thus Benjamin writes in this justly famous Thesis No. XIV: "History is the subject of a structure whose site is not homogeneous, empty time, but time filled by the presence of the now...it is a tiger's leap into the past. This jump, however, takes place in an arena where the ruling class gives the commands. The same leap in the open air of history is the dialectical one, which is how Marx understood revolution" (Benjamin 1985, p. 261).
8. I am following here Gershom Scholem's distinction between three versions of the messianic idea: conservative, restorative and utopian. See Gershom Scholem's "The Messianic Idea in Judaism" in *Messianic Idea in Judaism and Other Essays on Jewish Spirituality* (New York: Schocken Books, 1971), pp. 1-36.
9. Benjamin writes in this early text: "Historical time, however, differs from this mechanical time... a process that is perfect in historical terms is quite indeterminate empirically; it is in fact an idea. This idea of fulfilled time is the dominant historical idea of the Bible ; it is the idea of messianic time. Moreover, the idea of a fulfilled historical time is never identical with the idea of an individual time. This feature naturally changes the meaning of fulfilment completely, and it is this that distinguishes tragic time from messianic time. Tragic time is related to the latter in the same way that an individually fulfilled time relates to a

divinely fulfilled one." Walter Benjamin, "Trauerspiel and Tragedy" in *Selected Writings, 1913-26*, Vol. 1 (The Belknap Press, 2004), pp. 55-56.

10. "Theses on the Philosophy of History" in *Illuminations*, edited by Hannah Arendt, trans. Harry Zohn (New York: Schocken, 1985), p. 254.
11. Jacob Taubes, "The Price of Messianism" in *From Cult to Culture: Fragments toward a Critique of Historical Reason*, edited Charlotte Elisheva Fonrobert and Amir Engel (Stanford: Stanford University Press, 2010), p. 9.
12. Jacob Taubes, "Appendix A: The Jacob Taubes-Carl Schmitt Story" in *The Political Theology of Paul*, trans. Dana Hollander (Stanford University Press, 2004), p. 103.
13. "The Theologico-Political Fragment" in *Reflections*, edited by Peter Demetz (New York: Schocken Press, 1986), p. 312.

PART II

Reviews

5

Philosophy and Melancholy: Benjamin on Language and Truth

Ilit Ferber, *Philosophy and Melancholy: Benjamin's Early Reflections on Theatre and Language*, Stanford: Stanford University Press, 2013, 241 pp., $ 22.02 (pbk), ISBN-13: 978-0-8047-8520-4 (pbk).

I

Ilit Ferber's *Philosophy and Melancholy* is a much welcome addition to the Stanford series *Cultural Memory in the Present* edited by Hent de Vries. The book consists of a substantial introduction and four chapters: "Benjamin and Freud", "The *Trauer-Spiel*", "Melancholy and Language", "Melancholy and Truth". The book traces the idea of melancholy in the early writings of Walter Benjamin. Instead of presenting Benjamin's idea of melancholy either as a subjective-psychological-pathological mood or as social constructs, Ferber presents this singular idea in Benjamin as a potentially philosophical attunement (*Stimmung*), as *potentiality* itself that occurs at the intersection between the world and man. Ferber thereby withdraws from the dominant interpretation and understanding, not only of Walter Benjamin's idea of melancholy but of the idea of melancholy *as such*, melancholy predominantly understood as one pathological mood among others, as a subjective-solipsistic-psychological affectation or as social constructs (a "bourgeois" mood, one can say, which is the privileged indulgence of the dominant class). Reading the early works of Walter Benjamin in a Talmudic manner, the book introduces a debate, a *polemos* in our contemporary readings of

Benjamin and intervenes in debates concerning the relation of melancholy to the philosophical concept of truth, on melancholy as linguistic disclosure of the world and on the idea of melancholy as an ethical responsibility to the other. In other words, the book attempts to show "a metaphysics of melancholy" (p. 194) at work in early writings of Benjamin, an idea that touches and affects all other ideas at work in the early Benjamin: his notion of truth and language, of sovereignty and the political, of inheritance and ethical responsibility, of the spectral character of temporality and its relation to mortification, of the relation between play and work, of translation and sadness in language, etc. Therefore, melancholy for Ferber and for Benjamin himself is not one idea among all other ideas but one of those few ideas to be presented and which in turn *presents* – the world, man and the divine and their each time singular opening to each other. As Ferber makes clear through her careful exegesis of these early works that for Benjamin, especially for the early Benjamin, it is this *opening* of beings themselves (the divine, the mortal and nature) towards each other, each time occurring singularly and differently, that is at stake in the fundamental attunement (*Stimmung*) of melancholy. It is as if melancholy itself *attunes* each being toward the other; or, rather, beings themselves are disclosed in this attunement. In the very illuminating last chapter of the book, reading Benjamin in light of Leibniz's notion of harmony—evoking thereby that which is essential to music—Ferber shows us, contra the dominant understanding, that the Benjamin-word *Stimmung* is to be translated better as "attunement" rather than as "mood". As such melancholy is not one pathological mood among others, a solipsistic enclosure of the anthropological subject into its own interiority but *metaphysical* in the sense that such melancholy, as fundamental attunement (*Grundstimmung*), lies at the very *potentiality* of disclosures as such: of the divine, the mortal and of nature to each other in their unique, irreducible and singular modes. According to Benjamin's early conception of philosophy, it is the task and vocation of philosophy to let such "metaphysics of melancholy" arrive in the linguistic mode of presentation (*Darstellung*) which is philosophy, in so far as philosophy is the linguistic discourse par excellence and in so far as the fundamental attunement of melancholy adheres in language as such and language at all. For this early Benjamin, melancholy is something like a "secret password" that invisibly and continuously passes through all beings, demanding for an ethical response from us, the mortal, in whom this password reaches an innermost intensity of expression.

It is the merit of Ferber's *Melancholy and Philosophy* to let such a call of an infinite responsibility reach us through such a careful, loving and attentive reading of Benjamin. Bringing Martin Heidegger's early reflections on attunement (*Stimmung*) in proximity to Benjamin, and adopting his (Heidegger's) phenomenological mode of presentation to present the idea of melancholy as philosophical mood in Benjamin's early works, Ferber invites us to re-think melancholy in relation to philosophical task of disclosure and presentation. Such a re-thinking of a "word" or idea" through a presentation of it does not preserve its *sense* absolutely intact in the solidified, petrified mode in which it is displayed in the sedimented history of that idea, but rather transforms that very history into something new, something that is yet unheard and unseen. Ferber convincingly argues here that such is the case in both Heidegger and Benjamin. In each of these two philosophers the presentation of the idea or the word leads to the creative transformation of that history. In Heidegger's case, such creative transformation of the history of an idea occurs in the phenomenological disclosure of Dasein's own being opening its world; and in the case of Benjamin, such transformation occurs in the mode of presentation entering into a constellation of ideas. Therefore Ferber herself in her reading of Benjamin allows the idea of melancholy to enter into the constellation of Benjamin's other ideas, like the idea of truth (chapter four) and of language (chapter three), of death, of the spectral character of responsibility and the pain of its expression (chapter two). The work of Benjamin is thereby opened up once more for the reader, allowing him/her to encounter Benjaminian ideas in a renewed mode in a new context, the new context being the idea of melancholy as philosophical mood or as metaphysical opening of the world to the mortal.

Perhaps here lies the most important contribution of this book, not only to the reception history of Benjamin but to the larger debate concerning the relation of mood as such to philosophy and metaphysics, a debate in which melancholy assumes a very fascinating place. Ferber here justly points out the utmost relevance of Martin Heidegger's discussion of mood (*Stimmung*) to the contemporary debate on the relation of mood and philosophy. However, even though Ferber adopts the Heideggerian framework in her reading of Benjamin, her own discussion of the Heideggerian concept of mood remains limited and inadequate, her discussion being confined to his early works, basically *Being and Time* and his 1929/30 lectures on *The Fundamental Concepts of Metaphysics,* neglecting thereby the more profound reflections of the later Heidegger on the relation of melancholy to language, especially of poetic language (Heidegger's discussions of the poems by Stephan George and Friedrich Hölderlin) and on the relation of melancholy to thinking outside Occidental metaphysics (which is the task of his lectures called *What is Called Thinking?*). Perhaps the most important missing link here is Ferber's exclusion of Heidegger's 1934-35 lecture on Hölderlin's two hymns—"Germanien" and "Der Rhein"—wherein Heidegger understands melancholy as the *Grundstimmung* (fundamental attunement) of Hölderlin's poetry, and thereby hinting towards the possibility of thinking melancholy as the fundamental attunement of poetizing and thinking outside the dominant metaphysics of the West. Even though towards the end of the book Ferber returns to Heidegger again in order to substantiate her theoretical framework, the framework is still felt not substantiated enough and her approach still not sufficiently worked out. Taking into account these works by Heidegger, and showing of more profound proximity and distance between these two thinkers' reflections on melancholy would have not only enriched her theoretical framework but also would have more decisively placed the book in the wider debates concerning metaphysics, art, language and melancholy.

II

The decisive question here would be the following: how to think of melancholy as mood and of mood as such outside the framework of the Occidental metaphysics of the Subject? Reading Benjamin in light of the Heideggerian gesture of opening (of the dominant) metaphysics beyond its enclosures (subjectivist-psychological-egotistical and pathological), and taking the mood of melancholy as the guiding question, Ferber attempts to disclose that of melancholy which is unreleased in the history of that idea. According to Ferber, what Hegel is for Heidegger, the same is Freud for Benjamin. Therefore in Ferber's (and Benjamin's) reading of Freud's famous distinction of mourning and melancholia, Freud's reduction of melancholy into pathology (which, strangely, at the same time opens the possibility of thinking melancholy otherwise), functions somewhat like Hegelian *Aufhebung*: loss as the condition of possibility of work (which is the dialectical ruse of converting loss into work), interiorization (and preservation) of what is lost, an interiorization that constitutes the condition of possibility of the subject. Freud is rightly here considered by Ferber as the moment of disruption of the received history of the idea of melancholy and as the moment of inauguration of a new history associated with the birth of the discourse called Psychoanalysis. The decisive importance of Freud in the history of the concept must, therefore, be encountered. This is why Freud is important both for Benjamin and Ferber (she devotes her very first chapter to this juxtaposition of Freud and Benjamin).

Wherein lies the Freudian distinction between mourning and melancholia? It is the concept of "work": mourning makes itself available to work, to be worked upon it, to be converted into meaning, into the *symbolic* order of language. Its object can be assigned a place, a (de)nomination, a location and a signification. It is not for nothing that Freud calls it "the work of mourning" (*Trauerarbeit*) which as "work"—or rather as condition of possibility of work at all and of work as such—is not, strictly speaking, "pathological". On the other hand, the worklessness (or unworking) of melancholy is considered to be "pathological" by Freud: the psychoanalytical transformation of melancholy into "melancholia" (into a pathological condition) lies in this possibility and necessity of work whereby the subject can uplift (*Aufheben*; sublate) itself from a given loss into the inauguration of a new life.

Reading against this dominant discourse on melancholy, Ferber sees in Benjamin's early writings another, a "non-pathological" idea of melancholy. This non-pathological worklessness of melancholy in its utter unfathomable non-place between mute suffering and the discursive language of the concept and signification, between a cry and the language of music, remains at "the borderline" (a concept that Ferber borrows from Gershom Scholem), neither "this" nor "that", partaking both "this" and "that" at same time. Melancholy is, according to Ferber—and here the works of Jacques Derrida is important for her—*spectral*: neither dead (that is, complete annihilation) nor simply alive, neither mere absence nor presence, the spectre of melancholy is not even "afterlife" (unlike what the Romantics think of criticism). Not being able to die (nor being simply alive), the spectre of melancholy haunts the very *chronos* of being with a "dia" (namely, "apart"). Yet this diachrony is at the same time—and this is the paradox—the very condition of confronting the past at all. Ferber writes: "Benjamin curiously describes the world of spirits as "ahistorical". The ghost is ahistorical because it is entirely outside time; it is also, however, all about time and temporality. One way to comprehend this inherent paradox is to think about the distinctive temporal structure that Benjamin describes here: past and presence can exist diachronically, in parallel, only through an encounter with the ghost. In this structure the past does not necessarily appear at a moment before the present; it can coexist with the present and be gazed upon" (pp. 108-9).

The diachrony of melancholy is spectral: it can't be uplifted and sublated into (Freudian or Hegelian) "work"; it cannot be elevated into higher (the neo-Platonic concept of truth as non-material, non-sensuous) "truth"; it cannot be incorporated into symbol, into the language of judgment and signification via the conceptual logic of subsumption. The spectral-character of the (always already) lost object renders our melancholy incessant and without consolation. Hence is the melancholic refusal to give up materiality for the sake of a higher spiritual (one that is emptied of all sensuousness) "truth"; instead the melancholic devotes herself with complete fidelity to objects that materially present themselves to her in their disappearance. While all the time moving towards the language of music, melancholy betrays itself, fails itself on the *way*. Lament arises as this failure of/on the way, as this fragility and betrayal of language. The failure and fragility of the *way* never arrive at its work. The interiority of the subject is thereby never achieved completely without a remainder. The subject suffers here the most "ignoble" martyrdom for whom neither "this" world has retained its inherent meaningfulness (therefore lost its "place") nor has the transcendental beyond retained the power of its consolation and the promise of salvation. The utter desolation of this "worldlessness", this ruin of history which Ferber articulates so evocatively in her reading of Benjamin's *The Origin of German Mourning Play* in her second chapter, is the very worldlessness of the melancholic being. In her acute comparative reading of Benjamin with Freud here, Ferber shows us that the desolation and worldlessness of the Benjaminian melancholic is irreducible to the neat theoretical distinction of the psychoanalytical discourse (Freud in this case) between mourning and melancholia. The unfathomable, spectral character of melancholy for Benjamin destabilizes the neatness of the Freudian distinction in advance in the manner of "always already". Reading Freud in a deconstructive manner and at the same time thinking with his help, Ferber shows via Benjamin the possibility of thinking melancholy *before* the distinction between the work of mourning and melancholia as pathological mood. Reading another text of Freud from his later period, namely, *The Ego and the Id* (1923), Ferber shows that Freud himself later reconsiders this distinction he maintained in 1917.

While deconstructing the concept of work, Ferber however does not abandon the concept completely. Ferber locates in Benjamin's early writings another, if not a concept but an *idea* of work. The idea of work is now released from the Hegelian (who understands "concept" itself as work) work as concept or Freudian concept of it as constitutive possibility of the subject. As Ferber shows us in a very striking and illuminating way, the *passage or* the *way* of philosophical *work* for Benjamin is not *Strasse* but *Bahn*. For Benjamin, the task of philosophical work is not so much to overwhelm the object of thinking by suffocating it with the power and force of the sovereign subject with its intentionality but to release the object from the violence of the concept and thereby display it by presenting it as idea in a constellation. Far from subsuming the irreducible plurality and singularity of objects of knowledge under the generality of the concept, philosophical work is to display the truth content of these objects in a constellation of ideas which, instead of violating them, redeems them in turn. The *passage* or the *way* of the redemption of the object—which is the task of philosophical work—is not *Strasse* but *Bahn*. This passage is the way that the Benjaminian melancholic critic himself undergoes, the passage of mortification that the objects themselves go under so as to be redeemed. *Bahn* is therefore the passage of intersection or border between the melancholic critic and the objects undergoing mortification so as to be redeemed as ideas in a constellation. Therefore Benjamin recognizes a violence that lies in all works of intentionality initiated by the self-founding act of the subject. Far from being the property of the intentional subject that returns to its sovereign self-sameness, the *Bahn* of truth opens up for the first time to the redemption of the object. Hence is the remarkable remark uttered by Benjamin: "Truth is the death of intention".

A substantial part of the book is devoted to understand this enigmatic utterance of Benjamin: "Truth is the death of intention". Taking up two other philosophers apart from Freud, namely Kant and Husserl with whom Benjamin engages in *polemos*, Ferber shows how early writings of Benjamin attempt at releasing the idea of melancholy from the metaphysics of the subject. Thus Benjamin finds both in Kantian formal conception of experience as well as in Husserlian phenomenological notion of intentionality the violence and sovereign self-assertion of the subject. On other hand, melancholy for Benjamin is neither reducible to the empty experience of the Kantian subject (which is bereft of language and historicality) nor can it be reducible to the intentional structure of the phenomenological subject. Three philosophers (Freud, Kant, Husserl) or three discourses (Psychoanalysis, transcendental philosophy, phenomenology) are taken up by Ferber and she engages them in confrontations with or against Benjamin and shows thereby, by nuanced analyses, how for Benjamin the redemption of the object is the fundamental ethical task and fundamental stake in the attunement of melancholy. To show this, it is necessary to think melancholy outside the metaphysics of the subject. In threefold different manner the discourse of pathology (Freud), the discourse of transcendental philosophy (Kant) and the discourse of phenomenology of intentionality (Husserl) participate in the metaphysics of the subject. Against these discourses of the subject, Benjamin for Ferber opens up a philosophical discourse where not so much knowledge but truth, not so much concept but idea, not so much violence of the object via subsumptive logic of sovereignty but the redemption of objects in contemplation—that is at stake. The melancholic fidelity to the loss without minimizing, reducing or subsuming the loss into "work" (of mourning, of the concept, of knowledge and above all, of the subject) opens for us, according to Ferber's reading of Benjamin, to the ethical responsibility to the other. Loss is thus fundamental to the ethical responsibility. Bringing the works of Jacques Derrida (especially his book on Marx) into discussion on the questions of spectral character of mourning, of inheritance and being indebted and of responsibility as ethical opening to the others, Ferber reveals here the close proximity of Derrida with Benjamin. This part of the book I consider to be most beautiful.

III

It is an important contribution of Ilit Ferber (and of Benjamin) to introduce the problematic of language as fundamental to the attunement of melancholy. Benjamin understands melancholy not as a property of the subject's intentional structure (as in Husserl), neither in terms of Kantian empty experience (devoid of language and historicality) nor in terms of a pathological condition of an individual (as in Freud) but essentially the linguistic mode of disclosure of the (dis)continuum of beings—the divine, mortal and nature. Though the question of history is not taken up by Ferber (an important and perhaps necessary exclusion, given the tenor and focus of the book), the question of language is taken up in a big way. "Man's melancholy should therefore be understood" writes Ferber, "as inner linguistic, not psychological or subjective. Man is not sad or mournful for a specific loss relating to his subjective, contingent existence; his melancholy is linguistic, and it touches directly on his inability to execute his linguistic essence—that of naming nature"(p. 141). Benjamin thereby provides for Ferber an alternative "metaphysics" of melancholy, not the metaphysics of the subject but metaphysics that is concerned with the opening up beings in respect to each other *in* language as their communicating password. This password that makes possible the contiguity of beings (the divine, mortal and nature)—which Benjamin calls "the gift of language"—opens us to the messianic restitution of immortality. Benjamin calls it "pure language" or "the language of truth". It is the merit of Ferber's book to show that this linguistic structure of not only melancholy but of the contiguity of beings is reducible neither to the language-less mythic context nor to the intentional structure of the subject. It is therefore, according to Ferber, "Benjamin enthrones Adam rather than Plato as the father of philosophy. In Adam he finds a theological figure whose core is markedly linguistic than mythical" (p. 119).

From this astonishing statement three questions/problematic can be immediately elicited: 1. It appears here that Benjaminian discourse subjects to deconstruction the dominant Occidental (Greco-Roman) self-understanding of philosophy that sees Plato as the father; 2. What Benjamin (or Ferber) means by "the theological" is to be understood as the otherwise than "mythic", and 3. The question of language has a deeper relation to the theological than mythical. What at stake in these three claims is of immense importance for our contemporary thinking. Ferber, however, passes on without even raising these stakes as stakes and thereby neglects to formulate important consequences that she could have drawn from her insightful reading of Benjamin.

Language is Ferber's singular and the distinctive approach to Benjamin; it is here to be found the energy of her thinking. Therefore her reading of Benjamin—which is also Benjamin's style of reading—I call "Talmudic". In such reading language is constantly opened itself to its own *expressability* and communication opens to its *communicability* itself. Talmudic reading is oriented by a tendency of language to its own event, that is, towards its *potentiality*. The event of language is its potentiality which Benjamin calls "pure language". What passes, linguistically, through the contiguity of beings is this pure language as potentiality. Bringing Giorgio Agamben here into her discussion, Ferber understands Benjaminian notion of language as potentiality that by its innermost tendency opens itself to the expressability, the expressability that moves all expressions —from the mute, nameless creatures to the blissful melancholy that arises when Adam names them and from that blissful melancholy to its fall into the melancholy of overnaming when the naming language is transformed into the language of judgment. Thus the transformation of melancholy is for Benjamin the linguistic transformation par excellence which affects, in a fundamental manner, the very contiguity of beings.

What Ferber understands as potentiality, I understand it as the promise of language which is a messianic conception. It seems that the question of messianism—very fundamental to Benjamin—is not truly a fundamental problem for Ferber. It is this messianic promise that passes from the Adamic language of naming and of knowledge without concept (a blissful melancholy it is) to its possible messianic restitution to come. It is, however, not homogeneous continuity: the Fall of Adam and the building of the tower of Babel interrupt the immediacy of the former. Language then falls into prattle; the immediacy of knowledge is replaced by the language of judgment; the immanent magic of contiguity of beings is replaced by external magic of evil and the blissful melancholy of naming is replaced by the excessive melancholy of overnaming. Melancholy is thus a linguistic phenomenon; it is the *passage* between the divine, the mortal and nature. The messianic restitution of the naming language of man is opened in the abyss between blissful melancholy and the other melancholy, arising out of the violence of judgment and overnaming. Because of the possibility of the messianic restitution of justice to come (therefore Benjamin is also a thinker of future in an essential sense), the idea of melancholy is to be connected with Benjamin's idea of messianic happiness which, in the profane world, suddenly and in an incalculable manner, manifests itself—like the shooting star against the dark background of history that is in ruin. What I find missing in the book is a discussion on this relation that Benjamin makes between melancholy and happiness which for him are not incommensurable ideas but that which may belong together in their very diachrony. A discussion of this relation cannot evade the question of messianism in Benjamin's early writings, a serious question that I find missing in Ferber's book.

The question of promise brings Benjamin very close to Franz Rosenzweig's messianic understanding of language as promise which, passing through revelation, opens the world to redemption yet to come. Rosenzweig conceives such an immemorial promise as language before all (particular) languages, which is the potentiality of language as such and language at all, an idea very close to the Benjaminian idea of the gift of language. In that sense language is not only a disclosure of the world but an awaiting—for the eternity to come. It is again, as with Benjamin of "Language as such and Language of Man", the restitution-model of messianism that is at work. Bringing Rosenzweig in relation to Benjamin would have surely enriched the book and opened up new dimensions to her work. However, these limitations and missing links—the weak points of her work—may be, perhaps, it's very strength. I know very few books in our contemporary time which have so powerfully intervened in debates concerning mood as a linguistic and philosophical phenomenon. Despite these limitations, the book as it stands is still beautiful and an important contribution to some of the deepest concerns of our time.

6
Time, Language, Law

Franson Manjali, *Labyrinths of Language: Philosophical and Cultural Investigations* (Delhi: Aakar Books, 2014), 229 pp., 295 INR, ISBN: 978-93-5002-277-1.

Let me first congratulate Franson Manjali for his new book that bears such a fascinating title: *Labyrinths of Language*. The quotations from Ludwig Wittgenstein, given at the very beginning of the monograph, give us the sense of the labyrinths that are at work, not only in language as such but in Franson's own mode of thinking and working. Giving a title to a book or to a work of art always demands a genius unique and singular. In a certain essay, referring to Jean Luc Marion's unique talent to give titles to his works, Jacques Derrida dwells on what is at stake in a title, in entitlement, and the specific mode in which title bears its character as proper name. One day, but not today, I would like to discuss what is at stake in the specific mode of naming language that is giving a title: the secret, the crypt, the cipher or the code that a title must be and the aporia of this naming language: the sovereignty that is implied in each and every titles, and yet, the fragility, the precariousness, the provisional mode of each and all titles, whether the title of a book or the title that a political authority bears.

If one meditates a little more on Wittgenstein's idea of labyrinths of language, even if one dwells only on Franson's two quotations, one sees Wittgenstein evoking so many images of streets, paths, ways, and places, images always bearing the mark of plurality or multiplicity. Labyrinthine experience, for Wittgenstein, is somewhat like the linguistic experience par excellence whose topography is not experienced as calculable in advance, wherein each *topos* can be approached from multiple thresholds; an experience in which certain risk of having to lose oneself, and not having to know where one is, is inseparable. As if in speaking, one must risk one's knowledge, the knowledge of oneself.

One can't miss here his proximity, despite his differences in so many other respects, to the later Heideggerian thought on *Weg* which means, as we know, "way" or "path". We are grateful to Reiner Schürmann's great exposition of the later Heideggerian thought on *Weg* as a topography, as epochal constellation of presencing. If we read Heidegger backwards, like Schürmann does in reading Heidegger, and now I am trying to do that in respect to Schelling, we find Heideggerian *Weg* already announced in his phenomenology of *Wink* meaning beckoning or giving a *hint*. The excess or poverty, one and at the same time, of the phenomenological *Wink* of and below the predicative, propositional structure of occidental metaphysics is what is at stake in Heideggerian *Weg*. Thus the topology of the later Heideggerian idea of the epochal constellation of presencing consists of many ways, paths, and places and in streets which are each time incalculable and singular. Each *Weg* or path is taken out of a hint or a beckoning, a *Wink* that allows a glimpse to what escapes the epochs of beings. What escapes these epochs if not their fissures, their intervals and the phosphorescent apparition of their enigmatic mortality? Therefore, each possibility of a glimpse can only appear to us as instances of halt or arrest: when the epochs come to a closure, the constellation of presencing allows itself a glimpse in *Augenblick*, in the blink of an eye or in the lightning flash. In an entirely different register, and yet in certain proximity, Walter Benjamin too thinks this *Augenblick*, the *nunc stans*, as the messianic fulfilment of an index. An index is a code, a cipher, a crypt—that means, it is a secret password, bearing a promise of messianic fulfilment—implies *Weg* or a path to be taken. What Benjamin means by the present generation having to bear "the weak messianic power", by virtue of which the past has a claim upon us, is none other than having to bear the index or a secret password that enables us to welcome the past through the path of invisible, invisible because oppressed, history.

Wittgenstein, Heidegger, Benjamin: three different ways to think the way; three ways to think the title. The title "labyrinth of language" functions here something like a *Wink*, or index wherein the passage of thinking comes to an arrest, momentarily, to crystallize the nameless potentialities. It is the responsibility of the readers to release this potentiality, which I call "messianic", from its enclosures into sovereignties that is implied in the idea of entitlement as such. That means, we must release the messianic potentiality, implied in this index of temporality and language, from any nomothetic-hegemonic operation of language. The messianic potentiality is an index of temporality as much an index of language. That means, what ties up the enigmatic relation of time and language, is not just that each word or each sentence of a language ineluctably involves the grammatical marker called "tense relation", but rather, more enigmatically, it has something to do with the messianic potentiality itself.

As such, an index or a title always bears something excessive in itself: it bears the potentiality of messianic justice which is to be released, each time newly, from its exhaustion into law, into *nomos*. What releases language from being mere a nomothetic operation, an operation of *nomos* or law, is nothing other than it being an index, and it being *temporal* in a very fundamental sense. Each path is a new attempt to release such inexhaustive potentialities of language. When I try to see the relationship that this book might be bearing with other books and so many essays written by Franson, I don't see a fundamental thesis emerging from them but only ever new attempts to release that potentiality from all possible enclosures, from all nomothetic operations of the hegemonic order, as if as it were, his thinking can only be, by a logic internal to it, multiple and discontinuous attempts, and as though, the energy of his thinking can only be provisional and contingent, guided and nourished by the situation he finds himself each time, having to confront ever new enclosures and closures. As a result, he never appears to have given himself the task of drawing a large-scale picture of a book with a fundamental thesis underlying it. In that sense, Franson has never written a book, if the idea of the book demands certain exhaustiveness and certain fundamental principle or arché having to emerge from it and having a *telos* to aim for. It is *anarchic*, in the sense that Reiner Schürmann introduces it into our philosophical vocabulary. This weakness or perhaps that is his strength, makes him an excellent reader of texts: he reads tirelessly and comments on what he reads, like Benjamin or Heidegger or even Blanchot (these are the three great readers of texts that I know, and I must include the name Derrida).He reads the texts of Benjamin or Heidegger, Saussure or Blanchot, in order for them to come again to us, so that we confront them each in turn, so that an encounter can happen with these discourses, each bearing a proper name called "Heidegger" or "Blanchot". He thus bears something like a faith, which I suppose all readers of texts share, the faith that such encounters transform us, and such transformations must keep on going on indefinitely, as if it is nothing less than an infinite task itself. He reads the languages of these texts, all of these texts being texts of and on language, so that these texts confront their own languages and thus encounter their own excesses and surpluses. Each text thus becomes a labyrinth of language, that is, each text bears multiplicity of ways, points of entry bearing a password, and manifold points of exits, points that are never given to you beforehand, but must be discovered or recovered anew. A text is labyrinthine because the textile of each text is woven with paths, ways, streets and passages. This essential impatience reading, not having patience to constitute a system of propositions, is also a passage through which I see him passing, incessantly, by exchanging and yet retaining the password from door to door. I will just give you a very short list of these passwords to be found in this book under discussion; they are: time, messianism, law, literature, writing, death, sense, body, image. In each password, something like an obsession vigilantly watches over, almost like insomnia: Franson calls it, very simply, "language".

Yet this simplicity of language itself is so labyrinthine, consisting of so many secret ways, paths, streets and squares: that is the question that language poses itself to us, inviting us to release that potentiality of language, that is, the potentiality of unconditionality from all sorts of closures. Language, then, appears to be something infinitely much more than mere "language" with fixed and fixable grammatical properties, with attributes and predicates of logic, with categories and concepts of philosophy, with its communicational functionality at service of today's hegemonic order ruled by technology. That means, the question of language can't be merely the subject matter of one ontic academic discipline among others with its given methodological demarcation whose presuppositions and their condition of possibility that discipline itself is incapable of inquiring; language can only be a cipher to disclose the world as such in all its intrigue and depth, in all its manifold varieties and vagaries of existence. This is why I see Franson constantly grappling with the discourse that we have come to call, correctly or not, "post-structuralism", for what passes through this historical discourse is nothing other than attempts to release the world open from all possible closures and totalities, attempts in which language acquires the character of something like cipher or index, and not just one regional question among others. This is, if I am not wrong, Franson's unique task haunting him like an obsession over more than last 15 years; a task I said, and not a thesis, the linguistic task to open the world from all its nomothetic, hegemonic operations.

Let me take just one such index: "messianism". If we read Benjamin closely, we will see that the Benjaminian messianism is nothing other than an idea of "index" as such: one only need to read the second thesis of his *Theses on the Philosophy of History*, wherein Benjamin refers to the temporal index of the weak messianic power through which the past retains its claim upon us. I will not here report to you about what Franson has to say about messianism and the messianism of Benjamin. The essay, the fifth one of the book, called "Time, Language and the Destruction of Power" wherein Franson takes up Benjamin side by side with Bhartrhari's philosophy of language, is lucid and beautiful in itself, and demands attentive reading from us. I invite you to read this beautiful essay with the attention and care that it deserves. What I will do in the following few pages is to add a remark concerning what is at stake in messianism, especially in relation to the problem of time and language. Franson's text is a very uneasy text: the first part of the essay, devoted to Benjamin, rightly brings out the profound importance of language in the Benjaminian idea of messianism, especially his early essay called *On the Language as Such and On the Language of Man*, perhaps Franson's most favourite text from Benjamin as it is for me. The second part dwells on Bhartrhari's philosophy of language as he propounds in his *Vakyapadiyam*; it is here Franson brings out the profound relation that language has with temporality. In the first part, the question of temporality is not raised explicitly, but the question of the destruction of power is a fundamental problem there, which is in turn missed in the second part, at least in explicit terms. As a result, one has the feeling that one is reading two separate essays, somehow brought together, wherein one part echoes the other separated by an irreducible gap, like two lonely islands each one finding the resonance of its very solitude in the other, while solitude and foreignness itself remains as irreducible as ever before. Between the solitude of Benjamin, and the solitude of Bhartrhari: there is a translation of the untranslatable, and Franson here equally adheres to the other demand of translation, "don't translate the untranslatable", that is, "remain faithful to the irreducible and the singular".

I will discuss once again the question of language and time in the messianic light of intensity, and I will try to bring out the problem of the political. Perhaps the uniqueness of the messianic notion of language, especially that of Benjamin's messianism, is that language here is thought not only not as mere language with fixed and fixable grammatical properties and structures, with attributes or predicates of a subject, with categories of a cognitive system, let alone in its instrumental functionality of a communicative rationality, but also not even as mere "human". Language is more like an index of redemption which passes through history as a temporal event. Since redemption redeems not only "mortals" but the entirety of creation and nature, and it affects even the divine, language, therefore, far from being a property of "the human" subject—rather marks the very "contiguity of beings", the divine, the mortal and nature. "The contiguity of beings" is the phrase I am borrowing from my good friend Ilit Ferber who has recently published from Stanford University

Press a fascinating book on Benjamin. One can thus say that the very *expressability* as such—which Benjamin distinguishes from all given expressions—adheres in the very expressible being of these beings; in that sense, one can say, there is a linguistic being of nature as much as the linguistic being of the divine so much as the linguistic being of mortals. The promise of language is this expressability itself. We see that Benjamin names this expressability, which is an event of language and therefore has something essential to do with temporality, as "revelation". What, then, *Offenbarung* opens, or revelation reveals is no "this" or "that" expression; it reveals nothing, "no-thing" in that sense; it reveals this *expressability* itself which is no-thing. Benjamin therefore calls this "pure language", because it is no "this" or "that" language; it is pure language without means and without meaning. Analogous to it, in respect to the question of the political, Benjamin elsewhere refers to the "politics of pure means", that means, politics without means, and hence without goal. Paradoxically, it can also mean politics without politics, if all politics that we know them to be, is politics of means and end. A politics without means and without end, without *arché* and without *telos*, is anarchic politics in a very new, unheard and very profound sense, not anarchy that we generally know it to be. We now understand what Benjamin says, evoking Ernst Bloch, in his enigmatic *Theologico-Political Fragment*: messianism has only a religious sense, and not a political one; that means, there is no "messianic politics" as such, in its spirit and in its promise. This brings him very close to some of the unforgettable things that Franz Rosenzweig says towards the end of his *The Star of Redemption*: what passes through, from the originary word, which is no word but rather the potentiality of language or the promise of language, to the redemptive fulfilment with the coming of the Messiah, this passage is also the linguistic passage. In speaking, we wait: in speaking and in waiting, there is the event of temporality itself, for in waiting is involved the arrival of the Other from the extremity of time which is none other than future itself. We now understand the character of the index: index is the promise of the messianic future which is to arrive as the pure event of time.

This is, then, the messianic task of thinking and existing: to release this promise character of the index from enclosures in the language of judgment. With the event of the Fall, which is that of building the tower of Babel, the index-character of the index—Benjamin also calls it "naming"—becomes a means to an end. A language which is a means to an end is the language of judgment. Since in all judgment lays there violence, and the essence of violence, as Benjamin discusses in his *Critique of Violence*, is nothing but the relation of means-end in politics, the promise or the index of redemption withers away. As such the violence of the politics of means and end is bound up with the linguistic gesture bearing the character of a nomothetic operation. The *nomos* or law from which violence erupts is the metaphysical totalization of the verbality of the phenomenon into the nominative fixity via attributes, predicates, properties, etc. In other words, it is the metaphysical totalization of the pure language into the language of means and end. Reiner Schürmann's magnum opus, *Broken Hegemonies* thus brings the intimate relation between *nomos* and *nominative*: that all nomothetic operation of violence is a nominative totalization, of which he calls it "the hegemonic fantasm" of language. The messianic task consists of making fragile, of destituting or impoverishing the fantasm of language to release that verbality of the index that invisibly hints towards the pure language without means. What Franson calls "destruction of power", I will call it, non-dialectically, that is in a messianic manner—for messianism is without dialectics—I will call it destitution of power.

7
Theatre, Number, Event

Soumyabrata Choudhury, *Theatre, Number, Event: Three Studies on the Relationship between Sovereignty, Power and Truth* (Shimla: IIAS, 2013), 300 pp., 695 INR, ISBN: 978-93-82396-02-4.

The book is much awaited, especially for his privileged friends like me, friends who know that Soumyabrata has been working on a book for a long time. Some of us, and I am one among this "us", are fortunate enough to have had glimpses into the book in the process of its gestation and unfolding, a process from which certain "violence" is inseparable albeit a creative violence it is. Such violence seems to be inseparable from a book like this, given the formidable ambition and accomplishment of it, as we will be able to see now properly in the light of its publication. Such violence is audible in the very language of the work that does not welcome us immediately and the reader has to think a lot to decide whether she should pick up the book to read at all, not out of disrespect but precisely out of a profound respect, respect that we know to be a certain experience of distance or withdrawal. Such an "unattractive" or rather "attractive" quality of the book can be a disadvantage only if the book does not have such formidable ambition and is thus impatient in soliciting the reader's immediate attention and instant gratification. Sometimes such "indigestibility" or "unattractive" character proves to be good for the health of a work, especially if it merits serious attention from the reader who wants to read in a responsible manner.

Given the formidable character of the book that takes the reader into a labyrinth that seems to have a secret password connecting so many paths and counter paths, lanes and by-lanes and thereby weaving an intricate network of concepts, spaces, and times, it is impossible for me to talk about the book in a comprehensible manner. Moreover, one should leave the reader to the risk of the book, the kind of risk, or "wager"—a word that Soumyabrata is in love with—wager that book itself assumes. I should therefore let each reader to judge her/himself whether such a risk that the book undertakes is at all worth taking and whether the researcher has succeeded or failed in his attempt. I will just speak, within some minutes of clock-time, of one of the problems that book raises in a manner of a glimpse or in the blink of an eye. Obviously, it is going to be insufficient and even, perhaps, unworthy of me since I do different things, and raise some different problems in my works. So I will take up one problem, the problem with which the books begins, the problem that I am somehow more interested and slightly more connected, which is: the problem or rather the scandal of "sovereignty" and the question of the political-theology.

The question that Soumyabrata appears to me to have raised is not so much to ask: 'what is sovereignty or even, who is the "sovereign" so as to arrive at the "axiomatic" understanding of sovereignty or at the concept of the "political" as such. In fact, a good deal of the book is devoted to the even more preliminary discussion of the "axiomatic", bringing out carefully the precarious or fragility that adheres in the "axiomatic" as such, the poros or the aporetic that ties and unties its claims to the status of the "immemorial". The book rather raises the following uneasy question: 'Why is it that, and in what manner is it at all that the concepts/figures/modes of sovereignty assume the status of the "axiomatic" in such a way from which a certain claim of the "immemorial" is inseparable?' Now this assumption of sovereignty and this intrigue of the relation between sovereignty, axiomatic and immemorial itself, while being structural, is also historically variable, not just in a quantitative manner but in a manner of qualitative discontinuities. Thus from the liturgical foundation of sovereignty to the later Christus-Fiscus parallelism that justifies sovereignty, there is a discontinuity, in fact a violence that Soumyabrata delineates carefully with the help of Ernst Kantorowicz in a manner that will surely evoke much admiration for the reader. To answer the question he asks, Soumyabrata traces out a history or perhaps better, a genealogy of apparatuses of inter-linking practices and discourses alike by means of three interlinking fictions of concepts—"theatre", "number", "event"—to reveal the thread that tie and untie the "axiomatic" to the "sovereignty" and "sovereignty" in turn to the "immemorial". It appears here as if the porosity or fragility of the one immediately brings porosity to the others: the porosity and aporetic binding or unbinding of the axiomatic claims of sovereignty to the immemorial. Soumyabrata conceives that it is the philosophical task par excellence, the task of this strange discourse called "philosophy"—here I don't go too far with what he understands by "philosophy"—to envisage, or better welcome the "new immemorials" that are eventive, aleatory and ever new contingent eruption that breaks into the historical continuum of the world. Here and this now of this "breaking into" is the place of the "new", a space without a pre-given parameter of measurement and a time without pre-given measure of numbers. Such a possibility of thinking, for Soumyabrata, is given by a strange mathematics, now released from a dominant version of the "mathematizable" in the sense of the countable mathematics of number, a "contingent" or "situational" mathematics if at all one can use these words, mathematics that is not alien to "the logic of multiplicity" that constitutes and potentially deconstitutes each situation, each topos, each denomination, making hegemony of each and any nominative denomination broken. What, then, Soumyabrata seems to me to be concerned with are bruises, wounds or injuries that affect any claim of the worldly powers to sovereignty. If you read the text attentively in its performative gesture—and we all know that Soumyabrata is a great performer, a great actor—without hurrying to catch up with the core content or doctrine abstracted from the verbal character of the book, then you see these terms abound—especially the words like "wound" and "torsion", beautiful words they are, but also violent. For Soumyabrata, each axiomatic claim of the sovereign to the immemorial is wounded and is potentially broken, and by a strange logic, is marked by a paradox, by paradoxes, because these immemorials are never true immemorials. Therefore this discourse called "philosophy" needs to be infinitely restituted in the name of the "new immemorials" wherein immemorial has nothing much to do with something that has passed by beyond memory, but an immemorial, or rather immemorials to come which will never be part of any speculative memory and will therefore never be appropriable to sovereignty. This is his hope, and it is this hope and this promise that gives the energy and dynamis to Soumyabrata's thought. Insofar as such hope is unconditional, it can never be demonstrated or even validated by measures or numbers of what already exist as countable; they can thus only be "fiction", not "fiction" opposed to "truth" but "fiction" that do not need to oppose to "truth" at all, but rather welcome it, immemorial and infinite truth. Where, in what discourse, in what trembling language, in what tonality and gestures, in what rhythms and caesuras that such "fictions" may break into and be seized if not in "philosophy" itself, this abyssal and dizzying landscape wherein fabulization of the world may be taking place even though it is the very discourse that wants us to be disenchanted with the mythic foundation of the world?

Here comes the strangest paradox among all the paradoxes: philosophy alone is the discourse that, precisely by absolving from the immediate stakes of the world in an immediate manner of urgency—and therefore for philosophy alone such a task of the immemorial can at all be a task, a unique and so absolutely singular task—such a discourse alone in a profound manner exposes us to the absolutely contingent, so irreducibly aleatory and such precarious moments of life as they appear to us without any pre-given measurement of numbers and without the calculability of the "count as one". This is the problem of mortality. Soumyabrata has never raised this question in this manner, but he is so attentive to this strange paradox that ties and unties all sovereignty in advance. The sovereign must transcend any given situation that immediately exists as a generalizable order of law; as if the "halo of perpetuity", the term that he borrows from Ernst Kantorowicz, has never ceased to determine sovereignty as such, even if such a doctrine is historically applicable only to a specific formulation of sovereignty. But at the same time, mortality haunts each figure, each contour, each icon, each idol of sovereignty, bruising each figure with the wound of mortality. If so, the immemorial task of philosophy to welcome the "new immemorials" can only be bruised, wounded, and therefore a mortal immemorial, the immemorial that is haunted by the sting of mortality, with the possible death of the world. How to think this connection between mortality and the immemorial in such a way that each and every hegemony founded upon the sovereignty of principle—principle beyond all principles—is destituted, in so far as the question of sovereignty is essentially the question of principle, of thetic and thus is of the nominative?

I will conclude by taking you from Soumyabrata's book to another work. In the posthumously published magnum opus called *Broken Hegemonies*—a book that Soumyabrata has not referred in his work—Reiner Schürmann calls us to be attentive to the connection between thetic, denomination, nominative and nomos, a connection that establishes the an-archic arché of sovereignty, constituting thereby each linguistic regimes of hegemony. But mortality haunts each of such instituting and founding acts of natality, as if like an undertow, destituting each hegemony in turn and thereby rendering each situation, each historical condition tragic. Such a tragic is for Schürmann the true philosophical task of thinking that welcomes what he calls 'singularization to come'.

Perhaps the time has come to ponder anew over the tragic condition of our existence, one that is historical, in such a manner that we never cease welcoming such singularity to come, a never ceased destitution of all institutions in the name of such a 'to come'.

PART III

UN-CONCLUDING POSTSCRIPTS TO *THE PROMISE OF TIME*

8
Postscript 1[1]

This book titled *The Promise of Time: Towards a Phenomenology of Promise* is about promise, and it is about time and language. We immediately ask: What promise? To whom is it given? Who is it that gives promise?: Questions that are in dative, in accusative, and in nominative. You may change the order of questions as you like, beginning with nominative, and then accusative and finally to dative. There will be more questions, however, and I am sure there will be, questions like: what kind of giving is this that is giving of promise? Can promise be at all given? Does one give promise in the way, for example, one gives a slap, or a teacher gives marks to students, or like giving money to the poor out of charity? We can see that things are becoming more complicated, and we are not going into all that. Suffice it is to say that each time there are different modes of given-ness, and different modes of giving operating here, under irreducibly different conditions, and contexts that govern these performative gestures or acts of giving and receiving. They are conditional and conditioned promises, and conditional and conditioned giving.

The promise that we are concerned with here is not that sort of promise. Nothing, in the sense of 'no-thing' is given here, neither 'this' nor 'that' thing; yet it is not everything that concerns us, for we are definitely concerned with time and language. Promise is given, and promise is given to the one whose fundamental mode of his/her being is nourished by fecundity of time, and by nourishment of language. To such a being whose mode of very being is essentially temporal and linguistic, to him or to her is given time and language. As such, this promise and the given-ness operating in this promise here is not conditional or conditioned 'this' or 'that' thing. It can only be thought, which does not allow itself to be thought so easily, as unconditional and unconditioned. The promise of time and promise of language is thus not 'this' or 'that' promise but promise of promise itself, promise promising itself, promise that comes to give itself promise: the pure advent, or the pure arrival of promise as such, this arrival itself as such.

Such promise must be there—how to understand this 'there'?—already always the moment one opens one's mouth, and there language erupts, bursts forth, arrives or comes to presence; for only such an already always can promise language itself when one opens one's mouth. Along with language, time is simultaneously given as promise. It is not past, neither present nor future time. It is not 'this' or 'that' word in a particular language that a particular individual belonging to a particular linguistic community speaking, although it is true that one always speaks in particular language and particular words. Irrespective of whatever language one speaks and whatever words, there is always something (which is 'no-thing') like always already. One speaks here of an experience of desert or wilderness where one has not yet made a dwelling. The experience of time and language is like this. It is not yet past, present, or future time which are the three modes of time that allow something like the phenomenon of time to present itself to our cognition or to concept. We are speaking here of time and language that promises itself, and gives itself to itself. It is not a giving like any other giving which is always 'this' or 'that' giving; it is rather to be thought as giving itself, in its verbal sense and in its infinitive, which can never be thought as possession of 'this' or 'that' thing. Likewise the promise of time is never a possession of time of a subject or an internal consciousness, since it is not yet past, present and future in a sequence or series. What we are interested is this future anterior in the sense of its taking place which does not yet appear in time as this past, this present, or this future, yet they all arise from this taking place of time, from this coming to presence which has already always taken place the moment one opens one's mouth even before some word is uttered, which, having taken place, has opened itself to the indefinite, and indeterminate future: there then will be meaning, discourses, significations, etc. There is, as such, no discourse or meaning without this strange, enigmatic because inapparent already always, and not yet. In other words, to say with Derrida, there is no language without promise. I say, there is no time without promise. All language, and each language singularly is nourished by this promise of time, which is neither past, present nor future, but an already always which can only be discovered *a posteriori*, that is, in other time other than its own time. As a result we never posses time, for there is always other time, or to put it better, there is always otherwise than anything like 'our own time'. Time is never our 'own' time; we never exist in our own time: it comes from elsewhere, as a promise, as a pure givenness. This finitude, this non-possession is not an occasion of grief or despair; it is rather the very occasion of our hope and awaiting: that there will always be time, that there will remain time, that time will remain always. It is given to time that it will remain. It is the promise of time to itself.

This is in brief the idea of the messianic. For me the notion of the messianic is essentially the notion of promise. It is this promise that I see working in later Heidegger's very enigmatic formulation: "the phenomenology of the Inapparent". What can be inapparent if not promise par excellence? It is promise alone that while opening up time and language in each of its apparition, remains inapparent: it does not become past, present or future, yet remaining there everywhere as the moment of its advent and the moment of it's not yet. So that each time there is past, or present or future, there remains there that which does not yet appear as one point of a line among others. What is this inapparent apparition if not promise itself? If promise alone makes phenomena *phenomenal*, and if promise alone remains non-phenomenal amidst other phenomena forming a series, then such a phenomenology can only be "phenomenology of the Inapparent". And such a phenomenology is a phenomenology of promise. It is not phenomenology at all, if there are only phenomena which is adequate to their concept, namely, to their ideality so that there can only said to be phenomena which allow noematic-noetic co-relation to be without remainder. The inapparent character of promise, in its infinite fecundity of temporality, and in its essentially linguistic transcendence, asks us to think of a phenomenology in a very different manner. Not only temporality, no less important for us to consider phenomena like existence in its excess over all predication, freedom in its groundless character, and even death in its unthinkable advent that tempts us to console ourselves with Epicurus: "when death is there, I am not".

There is always something excess in our existence which does not allow us to totalize it in the immanence of our self-consuming predicates. Promise is such phenomenon par excellence, which I like to call 'unsaturated'. This insaturation is not an occasion of nostalgia or sorrow but our very reason for joy, for such excess alone can open our being to itself and to others, first of all and before any first. It is always therefore last after every last. This messianic idea is also an idea of justice. That there is time means there will be time for justice to be done to the unredeemed past sufferings. It thereby turns out to be the critique of the world. All acts of legitimization of worldly, profane power lose their force and justification because this justice speaks in the name of an absolute in relation to which any such theodicy of historical powers falls short of; they are rather appear unjust and unjustifiable. In the face of such tyranny of injustice, it is necessary to affirm such a transcendence of promise which is at once an intensification of difference. It does not matter too much whether such a promise which is promise of promise itself can at the end be called a phenomenology at all. What is necessary that through such a gesture an infinite movement traverses and will traverse an infinite chasm between the unconditional and the conditioned. Phenomenology turns out to be such an operational gesture and not a dogmatic school of possession by some thinkers want to call themselves 'phenomenologist'. If I still call forth such an operational gesture, it is because such a chasm interminably exposes us in the very midst of our everyday life, when one opens one's mouth for example, to such an extent that it is this chasm that may be considered the very *phenomenality* of all phenomena, and which is, strangely, the very non-phenomenon par excellence. You are, however, free to give it your own name. Anyway, that will also not be your name. Even 'phenomenology' is not its own name. It denominates something that exceeds itself. One can only say that each name is a sign-post showing direction to what it itself is not. Promise is such a sign post. This is the intricate connection between language and promise: that both are sign-posts. Their 'function' is to disappear in their fulfilment.

NOTE

1. These three texts are postscripts to my book titled *The Promise of Time: Towards a Phenomenology of Promise* (Shimla: IIAS, 2011).

9
Postscript 2

I

There are twofold movements of thoughts from which I draw inspiration for my work: on one hand a certain phenomenology wherein the *limit* of the *sense* of phenomenology itself is at stake, a paradoxical phenomenology, that is, a phenomenology based upon a paradox. I draw this paradox from a very unusual notion of phenomenology that occurs in Martin Heidegger's later work which he calls 'phenomenology of the Inapparent', a paradoxical phenomenology in the sense that it evokes a phenomenon which is no phenomenon at all, an impossible phenomenology in that sense. It is this 'phenomenology of the Inapparent' that has inspired the phenomenological works of Jean Louis Chrétien and Jean Luc Marion, among others. To a good extent my work is sympathetic to this phenomenological opening up of phenomenology itself beyond the eidetic phenomenology of Husserl, where the notion of the 'phenomenality' itself is raised again as the question at stake. The other inspiration is the messianic opening up of historical reason to a thought of redemption, nourished by the counter-dialectical resources of Schelling. 'The promise of time': this implies that time is the index of a messianic promise and fulfilment; it is the hinge that opens us to the plenitude of the infinite in its fecundity, allowing the infinity to measure us at the limit of our possibilities. This shows that I am primarily concerned with a promise which is an essentially messianic notion. Promise as I understand here is to be taken in messianic sense, or rather, messianic non-sense. It is contra-sense or non-sense in the way that the 'Inapparent' is paradoxical: it evokes an event that is not supported by concept, a phenomenon that is not exhausted by its actualization. I call it "unsaturated": phenomenon that cannot be saturated by any attributes or predicates. Such an "unsaturated" phenomenon can only be "tautology" (Heidegger): it occurs only once, as occurring only once, it can be said to be 'singular', for singularity, thought genuinely, is essentially a taulogical event.

Given this understanding, I would like to consider at the same time that this messianic notion of promise is other than one promise among other promises. It is the unconditional which the thought of messianicity is at all concerned with. Messianicity insists on the unconditional, otherwise it is not messianic. What arrives (*l'avenir*), arrives unconditionally. The coming of the Messiah is an unconditional arrival. It arrives when all our human possibilities and all our self-foundational acts of assertion and negation do not measure up to the unconditional demand of an absolute event that alone can bring redemption for us. It is this coming whose promise opens the world is the promise of time. The time of this unconditional coming is a time which does not occur *in* time. It is the moment, unsaturated in any predicative structure of language that seizes us and dispossesses us. What I call "ethics of finitude" is concerned with an event whose effect precedes its visibility in concept; whose eventiveness precedes its apparition in cognition. Messianic is concerned with such an event. As such, messianicity speaks in the name of an absolute or unconditional eventiveness that refuses to be recognized in any epochal or historical manifestation that can be grasped in the world-historical narratives. To put in a more negative manner, messianicity puts a question mark to the entire domain of the historical, the entire world of human 'possibilities'. It interrogates all acts of legitimization on the part of any, each and every worldly power in the profane world. In that sense, messianism is the thought of the 'impossible'. It is the distress of waiting for an arrival at the limit of human possibility; or, conversely, it is the hope for an arrival at the extremity of catastrophe. In the face of this arrival which is *to come* from such an extremity of time, all human power loses the force of its justification. Messianism is the suspension of law. Beyond the force of law and the gaze of power, messianism affirms that which never stops withdrawing from us, that while withdrawing from our gaze, gives us justice at the limit of our possibility, of our capacity, of our force and of our power.

The promise that is without being 'this' or 'that' promise is not therefore some abstract or empty promise. In order to open up such a thought of the promise of time, it is necessary: 1. to release the notion of the event and time from their subjugation to ontology, the classical ontology as that which determines 'being as presence', and 2. It would be necessary to put into question the metaphysical ground of history as such. Who but in Hegel does such an ontology of history find their metaphysical fulfilment? The messianic attempt to open up the closure of the immanence of history, a messianism so very influenced by the works of Franz Rosenzweig, has to be nourished by the counter-dialectical movement. Hence is the importance for me of Schelling's and Heidegger's non-dialectical opening to the event of disclosure that is pre-predicative, a disclosure that is the *donation* of phenomenon itself, the unconditional gift that while granting us phenomenality, withdraws from all given presences. Can this inapparition be considered, then, other than as 'promise'? Now this is the thrust of the whole argument which I took pains to show: the phenomenology of the Inapparition is nothing other than phenomenology of promise itself, promise in messianic sense of a structural opening of the world, as the event of disclosure that will henceforth mark all phenomena of the world as a pure gift of being. At the beginning of the world lies promise. The whole domain of language opens in this promise at the very moment one opens one's mouth—even before concept and prior to knowledge—and there is, lo, promise itself! 'That there is promise': this is an inapparent occurrence. It is an event before being; an opening before any predicates. Such promise is 'there' even before anything is promised; rather, it is the 'there' itself with which each entity of the world presents itself to us in language. One can say that such promise promises itself; it promises all presences in advance before anything being presently present. Such promise promises fulfilment which is not fulfilled in the worldly powers of the profane order, or in the immanent self-presence of our history. In the world that is constituted by "law positing and law preserving violence" (Benjamin), the promise is not yet fulfilled. Hence is the necessity, promised by promise itself: that there must remain a time to come beyond the work of death, beyond the violence of history, beyond the gaze of law. Such time is no time; it is not a time that serves death, that is subjugated to the world-triumphant march of history, or that is constituted by the force of law. No, it is not such a time at all, but a time that opens to infinity and eternity, an eternally remnant of time, an eternal remainder of time. This remainder of time is time always *to come*. It comes from an extremity of time, at the *Eschaton* of history, from a future in an infinitive sense of the verbal. The promise of time is this promise: that there will be time after each and every end, because it is at the very opening of the world, because it has begun before any beginning. Only then may there be justice which is not possible within the immanent world of the historical reason. To have time means to have time for justice, time that justice itself demands that everything is not yet finished, that there is always a remnant—a 'not-yet', *Noch Nicht* (Bloch) which is not yet a *topos, being deprived of habitation and a name*, hence is utopian. This time does not allow to be thought on the basis of death, rather death is to be thought on the basis of this time (Lévinas). This is the crux of the messianic notion of the promise that I am attempting to think.

II

The question of history is one of the fundamental concerns of my work. Against the immanence of history which is grounded metaphysically by Hegel's speculative dialectics, messianism rises up with the promise of an eternal remnant of time. Hegel's speculative-dialectical understanding of history, history that is led by its immanent, irresistible force of the negative to a determinate *telos* is only a secularized version of the theological, a theodicy of history. Reduced to an immanent, determinate movement of history, eschatology loses here its tremendous intensity of inspiring the oppressed. In fact the eschatological intensity is here made to serve as finalism in the name of which sufferings, injustice and oppression in the past are passed off as necessary for the sake of, and in sight of its finality that never arrives. Messianism is a refusal of such finalism; instead it evokes, in the name of justice for the oppressed, of an eschatology or messianicity without finalism, an *Eschaton* that would not be part of the immanence of history. Now this is an impossible idea conjured up by messianism: it demands, in the name of justice, an end which is without finality and without end; or rather, it is the end after each and every end; or, even better, it is the hope of an *Eschaton* that must open up time beyond the whole of history. It is the apparition, then, which is truly and genuinely inapparent, in the sense that it is not visible *in* the time of time, and *in* the time of history. Messianism is this demand of a wholly otherwise notion of event than the dialectical version of the event that occurs in the immanent plane of history, belonging to human possibility and marked by the violence of law.

In this book I have attempted to think such a notion of the event with the help of Hölderlin. The non-dialectical notion of the event is a "monstrous copulation". Instead of thinking the event as belonging to the speculative unity of the Subject, such event must—in its sudden eruption—bring together in an agonal manner the end and the beginning, joy and melancholy, time and eternity, simultaneously and at the same time. What I am, then, trying to think is not events that are periodic breaks belonging to the metaphysical principle of identity whose unity is guaranteed by the historical becoming of a speculative subject. I have identified the logical principle of identity as what Hegel himself calls in the Preface to *Phenomenology of Spirit* as "speculative proposition" which is none but a predicative proposition, in the sense that speculative proposition seeks to recount, retrospectively, what has already happened. The event which arrives to us from the extremity of time, in the sense of its future anterior, does not thus allow itself to be thought on the basis of predicative proposition. Rather such an event is this radical epochal break itself where the entirety of history is consummated at a momentary halt. The monstrosity of this event, because it does not belong among other events to the line of successive, periodic events, this epochal break can only be an impossible event, because it unites simultaneously and not successively, at the same time both the end and the beginning, the eternity and time, melancholy and joy, death and life. For me, such an impossible event is the event of the messianic arrival that seizes us while dispropriating us and exposing us to our finitude. That eternity may arrive today, even now, just at this moment when I am reading this line: this possibility is an impossible possibility. Only messianicity realizes this unrealizable, and makes possible the impossible. This event, then, does not belong to the dialectical history, for what is dialectical history if not the domain of the possible? In such a dialectical march of world-historical politics, the end is postponed indefinitely to the end of a line and located at the end of a series. Messianism, on the other hand, de-formalizes time as succession of instants, so that the eternity, which is nothing but an extremity of a radical future, may erupt *here and now*. That this 'now' may be eternal or, the eternity may be presencing 'now': this "monstrous copulation" is the copulation of past and future, at this moment, at any moment, as a 'perhaps'. So the past may come in the future and the future may have already arrived in the past. This is the messianic possibility which is the very possibility of justice, as the keen readers of Walter Benjamin know. The past injustice that demands messianic justice must conjure up an impossible event that must erupt contra all the believable logic of time as a series of successive instants. That past may come again and may be lived again in a time to come: this alone may render justice to the past sufferings of the vanquished. The promise is this promise of a time when the past has not yet inevitably passed by without remnant, contra all logic of time, and contra all logic of promise—an impossible time and an impossible promise. The world-historical march of dialectical movement, on the other hand, is based upon the inevitability and necessity of the past that must have passed away. The past that has not yet passed by can alone be the eruption of the unconditional. It does not belong to the determinate order of the necessary and inevitability of the succession of quantifiable instants. A past that remains past without having passed by is the inapparition that invisibly keeps opening up the domain of the historical and the profane. As a result, the theodicy of history cannot draw its justification from its immanent forces. The domain of the world-historical politics must be judged by this ethical which is given by the unconditional demand of justice. This ethics is the unconditional ethics of redemption. It is redemption that invisibly, *inapparently* passes through history as a secret password, or as a secret index that alone can justify the historical reason. It is in this sense promise is essentially ethical which is to be thought neither on the basis of the Kantian regulative principle nor the basis of Hegelian dialectical theodicy of history. The true eschatology evokes the ethical as de-legitimization of each and every attempt of sovereignty in the profane order of world-historical politics. The idea of promise is thus not a beautiful, aesthetic, harmless concept that gives rise in our heart with immense hope and enthusiasm for lots of grand world-historical triumphant politics. Born out of the deepest catastrophe, it is given to the distress of those who are oppressed by history and by the world-historical politics. This thing called 'promise' is also a suspicion. It keeps insomniac vigilance over each triumphal cry of victory that is heard in distance or nearness. They all for such promise fall short of the absolute and the unconditional. The insufficiency of all that is a human possibility, and *that redemption does not occur at the level of world historical politics*: this is the presupposition of messianism. While this is the source of messianic distress, and this is also the very same source of messianic hope.

III

The event that does not belong to the determinate order of the irresistible march of necessity must be an *offering* of freedom, for what is freedom if not another name of the unconditional? It is this question that primarily I dwell in the third part of the book, drawing primarily on Schelling. The messianic potentiality of Schellingian thinking is thus brought out again, inspired here by the two very important messianic Schellingians: Ernst Bloch, and Franz Rosenzweig. The ecstatic vision of a past that never ceases groundlessly and immemorially opening up the world, and which for that matter never becomes a passed past: this "irreducible remainder" (Schelling), this eternal remnant of time that always ceaselessly exposes the immanence of history to the *Eschaton* arriving from an extremity of time—is not this messianic vision of history par excellence? 'The ages of the world' is opened by a ground that never itself be grounded again. How we can we name this abyss if not 'freedom' itself, freedom that never ceases opening us to the immemoriality of promise on the one hand, and to the eschatological arrival of eternity from the extremity of time on the other hand. At once, and this is the greatest contribution of Schelling, all immanence of the theodicy of history is immediately brought under question. The question of freedom is thus based upon a strange paradox or aporia: the ground of condition cannot itself be grounded again. It is this aporia that un-works in advance any constitutive possibility of system, and more specifically that of the idealist system. As a result, the ground remains an indigestible, excluded remainder that never ceases haunting each and every human 'system' or attempt at 'totality'. It is something like the Benjaminian past: the dead is never 'dead', and never yet finished, for they never stop claiming for justice in the world where the victorious always assumes injustice in the name of law of history, in the name of finalism of progress, in the name of grand world-historical politics. Schelling's eschatology evokes an abyss of freedom that never ceases giving the mortals the gift of being, even though the possibility of a radical evil marks the very being of such being, because of its irreducible finitude. I see here the most fascinating thought of promise. Schelling here evokes the possibility of a radical evil that never ceases threatening our historical existence. Hence is the melancholy of history that arises out of freedom, a fundamental melancholy that touches even God, let alone the mortals. Where then does evil arise? Evil arises when the mortals to whom his/her being is gifted by an inscrutable freedom turns up against his very created-ness, and wants to be God-like; he attempts to found the kingdom of the divine on the profane order by the force of his all too human law. He forgets thereby that freedom can only be at best 'loaned' to him that marks the insufficiency of all that is of the mortal. History can be none other than a realm of this apostasy. The moment such an apostate condition attempts to assume divine sovereignty, all hell is let loose on earth and there occurs dissolution of the world. History then becomes diseased. What is evil if not a spiritual disease? There can arise evil only where there manifests history. As an apostasy, history belongs to the gift of freedom, and not vice versa; for there must *already* sway the groundless open-ness of freedom for there history to manifest itself at all. The arrogant and triumphant attempt at the theodicy of history brings dissolution to the nexus of beings, and there evil, which is otherwise always possible, manifests itself as actual. The melancholy of the mortals is therefore also the saving grace. Schelling here brings out this question decisively at the end of his *Freiheitschrift*. If melancholy exposes the finite mortals to the non-appropriability of the gift of freedom, this precisely constitutes the promise of beatitude, the promise of redemptive joy. The messianic hope for redemption is essentially *daimonic* in both senses of the term: it is demonic or monstrous in Hölderlinian sense, and it is 'daimonic' in Platonic sense where 'daimonic' also signifies happiness or beatitude. The gift of beatitude or daimonic joy arrives to us when the mortals learn to renounce the appropriation of freedom that alone grants them the gift of being. The mortals must first of all learn to be abandoned, even by God and by everything and everyone else. To learn to be abandoned is to be exposed to the gift of an excess whose time and space will never be grounded in the immanence of our self-presence. Such a gift, beyond all human possibility, arrives from a destination wholly otherwise, from another site and another time. To such an abandoned, exposed being the promise is also given: that there will always remain a time to come, that there will be the eternal remnant of time, that eternity is given to us that may erupt today or tomorrow. The arrival of eternity is the messianic moment of beatitude or joy that arrives unconditionally, that means, out of a groundlessness of freedom as a sublime offering.

In my ongoing research work which I call tentatively *The Political*

Theology of Schelling, I hope to work towards a critique of historical reason from this Schellingian transcendental-theistic point of view. This critique is an interrogation of the immanent closure of such a historical reason that assumes the form of theodicy to justify and legitimize the embodiment of the divine on the earthly power in the profane order. The gift of beatitude, thus, does not occur in the immanent plane of history. It rather arrives from a destination that does not allow to be embodied without remainder in any of the 'figures' of the profane order. The whole endeavour of Schelling's later philosophy is how to think and envision the possibility of redemption precisely on the basis of that which makes the human non-autarchic and non-autochthonous, that renders each product of the human, even the modern state, into that which must pass away, although precisely by passing away it opens to the divine excess, to the possibility of the "second covenant" that alone redeems the world. This demands abandonment of all triumphalism through infinite acts of mortification of ego, or renunciation of any totalizing claim that absolutizes that which must merely pass away and of all that is mere potentiality without actuality. Only the divine is that "actuality without potentiality", in that, it alone is that which does not have any other predicates other than itself. The attempt to establish this divine excess which is "actuality without potentiality" in the immanent plane of the apostate world without regulation of the divine excess would immediately throw the world into abyss or dissolution. Hence is the necessity of *Gelassenheit*, an idea that I have borrowed from Meister Eckhart, later used by Heidegger: mortification of all force and all potencies of the world in the face of that demonic excess of actuality. Only then mortal can partake in the divine excess, not on the basis of power and force of the human which is nothing other than mere potentiality, but on the basis of non-power, or renunciation of all power in the face of the divine. Understood in this manner, Schelling's eschatology is a critique of each and every power that operates in the immanent plane of history. This disjunction and caesura, but not opposition, between these two modes of existence, makes the analogy of the divine and profane impossible. But this is not merely a negative gesture but only the negative side of a far more affirmative gesture: the affirmation of an ethics of Good beyond being that alone consummates history. This is the direction that I perceive that my present research is going to take, relating my work to philosophers like Jacob Taubes and Søren Kierkegaard: very important thinkers for me.

IV

If the event of arrival does not allow itself to be predicated in the categorical grasp of concepts, in so far as the categorical apparatus can only grasp entities "present at hand" (Heidegger) and not the event of *presencing* itself, language then itself must be thought in a more originary manner, not primarily in its predicative function but as pure exposure, in a lightning flash, to the event of presencing which is the inapparent par excellence. Hegel's dialectical determination of language as essentially conceptual is again the adversary here. In so far as Hegel's dialectical-speculative notion of language subsumes language in the service of a speculative universal, language here is reduced to its cognitive disposal. In the second part of my book, the attempt has been made to think language as the non-negative finitude that affirms what is outside dialectical-speculative closure, the event to come. Language here is thought in its promise character. The promise of language lies in its opening up of the world before and prior to any categorical grasp of the concept. This originary disclosure of language, not yet impaired by the violence of cognition, alone carries the possibility of a redemptive fulfilment. How to think this messianic promise of redemption, given in language, even before there is categorical grasp of "entities presently given" if not as the event of denomination itself? Such language is not a means of communication of entities within the world but the disclosure of the world, of what I call *worlding* of the world, which does not allow to be used as the representational act of the Subject at the conceptual disposal. As the language of the event of pure denomination, this messianic promise of language is *presentation* itself, in the German sense of the word *Darstellung,* presentation of nothing other than *presencing* itself. A tautology which marks the 'Phenomenology of the Inapparent': it presences presencing itself, and nothing other than that, and therefore *presencing* only once. Language is primarily, then, this pure event of presentation that presents in poetic saying rather than in cognitive categories. The possibility of such language marks redemption of the world and the restitution of the messianic beatitudes whose possibility is given in the very fact there is language. Rosenzweig calls such language *silence* which is not the reticence of speech by the death defying tragic hero of the mythic world, but where language fulfils itself in beatitudes, while granting us the gift of being present to oneself.

It is the poetic saying rather than the conceptual language at cognitive disposal that summons, as in a lightning flash, the event of pure presencing. The event presenting purely itself in 'actuality without potentiality' strikes us, in the manner of Hölderlin's speaking of Apollo striking us, with a lightning flash when eternity conjoins with time, and joy and melancholy, birth and dissolution unites in a "monstrous copulation". What is poetic saying, then? The poetic saying is nothing other than place of encounter, not the place as 'this' or 'that' place, but *placing* of all places, the place that first of all places any place, where the encounter takes place, happens, occurs, the *taking* place as *such*. In other words, it is the very *taking* place of history *as such*, the opening or inception or inauguration of history itself, rather than what belongs to the domain of the immanent plane of history. This is for me the true and the genuine notion of the event. It is this which is the inapparition par excellence. Thus when I say that I am not concerned with 'this' or 'that' coming but the very *coming* itself, it is this *taking* place of history itself. This can never be grasped in the conceptual apparatus of predicative categories. It can only be welcomed in the poetic saying, on the basis of renunciation of all appropriation, of all power and of all mastery. The event of pure presentation rather dispropriates us beforehand, and marks our forehead with the irremissible mark of mortality. "The ethics of finitude" has to do with the gift of eternity that arrives to us only on the basis of our mortality and of our dispossession. Mortality, far from being an event of annihilation, alone grants the possibility of existence for the finite being. Only such a being whose very being is a gift, can partake of the divine excess, that is, in beatitudes, as gift but not as possession. That demands that the highest task of the mortals is to release this transcendence from its imprisonment in "the cages of the world" (Jacob Taubes). Messianism seeks interruption of the immanence of history and suspension of law so that the unconditional may not be imprisoned "in the cages of the world". The philosophical task of my own work has been nothing other than to release the unconditional from the various immanence of self-presence.

V

I conclude with a few words about the *way* of my research. The book does not aspire to be a system nor does it follow a method which is an imperative for any academic research. Thus phenomenology here is a certain mode of presentation (*Darstellung*): differential presentation of singulars in a movement of constellation, an idea that links this work with the philosophical orientation of Rosenzweig and Benjamin. What we are attempting to think with the notion of configuration, or constellation is a whole without totality, an assemblage without system. A conceptually and logically generative principle running through them does not unite them, nor are they inserted into the cognitive apparatus of categories. The configuration movement, insofar as this movement inaugurates the singular coming into existence and not what has already been predicated in the generalized economy of system, has to be thought outside such a system. The generalized economy of the categories miss the event—the event of coming—it is because it subordinates the thought of configuration to the system and to totality, the lightning flash of language to concepts, transcendence of a presupposition to the immanent generation, existential constellation to categorical thought, the naming language of the mortals to the *apophantic* grasp of "presently given" entities. The traditional methodological principles of the distinctions between praxis and theory, content and form, and a progressive movement of knowledge production, deductive or analytic, that concludes with a determinable result: all these are set aside for the sake of a mode of presentation where differential pathways of opening to truth is displayed, in a gesture of repetition, in a constellation or configuration. What is at stake in this whole endeavor is raising the question of philosophy itself. If this book can still be called 'philosophical', it is not by the conventional standard of 'academic' research pursued in universities nowadays, but rather in the old, Platonic sense of the philosophical: that the astonishment, wonder or exposure to the coming of truth is primarily an *existential* import, which I consider to be far more originary phenomenon than the categorical grasp of entities at the service of conceptual disposal. The philosopher, in the Platonic sense, would be nothing other than a "perilous being", being whose very being is in peril, someone who puts his very being in risk in the voyage to the unknown, thereby exposing himself to the demonic weather of the sea, and to the tempestuous waves. The philosopher is a monstrous being, a demonic existence as Socrates never forgets to remind this for us, whose monstrosity lies in philosophy's ceaseless conjuring up of the unfamiliar and strangeness into the world that otherwise appears domestic, inhabitable, and familiar. Retrospectively as I think of the book, it is appears to me above all that it is a deeply Platonic text.

10

Postscript 3

A REJOINDER TO ARINDAM CHAKRABARTI[1]

I

First of all, I must thank Prof. Chakrabarti for being kind enough to take up the book to read. The book review does not even bring to disclosure what the book is all about, what is its fundamental stake and where does it intervene—a task every serious book review ought to fulfil. Instead the book reviewer devotes a substantial part of the review to the Kantian notion of hope and Indian Karmic theory which do not have anything substantial to do with what the book is all about. Then the book reviewer simply goes on to dismiss the book on grounds that simply convey that he has not even cared to read the book. A patient, serious reading—a reading that generously opens to a thought that is unfamiliar and different without bringing it back to the familiar, closed ground of oneself—such a responsive and responsible reading discloses the different mode of argumentation and different stakes of the book that one is reading. This rejoinder is a response, not so much to the misreading of the book but to the non-reading of the book. After reading the review by Prof. Chakrabarti, I felt that a statement of clarification is necessary concerning the stakes, the content, the mode of argumentation of the book, not so much to determine beforehand the possible readings to come, but to partly to open the book for the reader once more and partly to respond to Prof. Chakrabarti himself.

II

The book draws its inspiration from two fold movements of thoughts: on one hand a certain phenomenology wherein the *limit* of the *sense* of phenomenology itself is at stake, a paradoxical phenomenology, that is, a phenomenology based upon a paradox. I draw this paradox from a very unusual notion of phenomenology that occurs in Martin Heidegger's later work which he calls 'phenomenology of the Inapparent', a paradoxical phenomenology in the sense that it evokes a phenomenon which is no phenomenon at all, an impossible phenomenology in that sense. It is this 'phenomenology of the Inapparent' that has inspired the phenomenological works of Jean Louis Chrétien and Jean Luc Marion among others. To a large extent my work is sympathetic to this phenomenological opening up of phenomenology itself beyond the eidetic phenomenology of Husserl, where the notion of the "phenomenality" itself is raised again as the question at stake. The other inspiration is the messianic opening up of historical reason to a thought of redemption, nourished by the counter-dialectical resources of Schelling. "The promise of time": the title implies that time is the index of a messianic promise and fulfilment. Time is not thought here in Kantian manner as an *a priori* form of intuition, but in a messianic manner in its verbal resonance, time in relating itself to a thought of history in a counter-dialectical mode (hence beyond or outside Hegelian mode). Unfortunately, Prof. Chakrabarti does not even touch the most basic problematic of the book, despite it is already made clear in the very introductory chapter of the book. Instead, Prof. Chakrabarti goes on to speak of 'San Francisco-based feel good guru', immediately after mentioning Kant, avoiding the fundamental intervention that the book seeks to introduce in the discursive world.

Time here is considered neither in the Kantian manner as *a priori* form of intuition nor in the Hegelian manner as dialectical but in a messianic manner, influenced by Franz Rosenzweig, time as the hinge that opens us to the plenitude of the infinite in its fecundity, allowing the infinity to measure us at the limit of our possibilities. This shows that I am primarily concerned with a promise which is an essentially messianic notion. Promise as I understand here, is to be taken in the messianic sense, or rather, messianic non-sense. It is contra-sense or non-sense in the way that the "Inapparent" is paradoxical: it evokes an event that is not supported by concept, a phenomenon that is not exhausted by its actualization. I call it "unsaturated": phenomenon that cannot be saturated by any attributes or predicates. Such an "unsaturated" phenomenon can only be "tautology" (Heidegger): it occurs only once, as occurring only once, it can be said to be "singular", for singularity is, thought genuinely, essentially a tautological event.

Such messianic notion of promise is other than one promise among other promises. It is the unconditional which the thought of messianicity is at all concerned with. Messianicity insists on the unconditional, otherwise it is not messianic. What arrives (*l'avenir*), arrives unconditionally. The coming of the Messiah is an unconditional arrival. It arrives when all our human possibilities and all our self-foundational acts of assertion and negation do not measure up to the unconditional demand of an absolute event that alone is redemptive. It is this coming whose promise opens the world is the promise of time. The time of this unconditional coming is a time which does not occur *in* time. It is the moment, unsaturated in any predicative structure of language, that seizes us and dispossesses us. What I call "ethics of finitude" here is concerned with an event whose effect precedes its visibility in concept; its event-character precedes its apparition in cognition. Messianic is concerned with such an event. As such, messianicity speaks in the name of an absolute or unconditional eventiveness that refuses to be recognized in any epochal or historical manifestation that can be grasped in the world-historical narratives. To put in a more negative manner, messianicity puts a question mark to the entire domain of the historical, the entire world of human "possibilities". It interrogates all acts of legitimization on the part of any, each and every worldly power in the profane world. In that sense, messianism is the thought of the "impossible". It is the distress of waiting for an arrival at the limit of human possibility; or, conversely, it is the hope for an arrival at the extremity of catastrophe. In the face of this arrival which is *to come* from such an extremity of time, all human power loses the force of its justification. Messianism is the suspension of law. Beyond the force of law and the gaze of power, messianism affirms that which never stops withdrawing from us and that, while withdrawing from our gaze, gives us justice at the limit of our possibility, of our capacity, of our force and of our power.

The promise that is without being "this" or "that" promise is not therefore some abstract or empty promise. In order to open up such a thought of the promise of time, it is necessary: 1. to release the notion of event and time from their subjugation to ontology, the classical ontology as that which determines 'being as presence', and 2. It would be necessary to put into question the metaphysical ground of history as such. Who but in Hegel does such an ontology of history find their metaphysical fulfilment? The messianic attempt to open up the closure of the immanence of history, a messianism so very influenced by the works of Franz Rosenzweig, has to be nourished by the counter-dialectical movement. Hence is the importance for me of Schelling's and Heidegger's non-dialectical opening to the event of disclosure that is pre-predicative. It is the event of disclosure that is the *donation* of phenomenon itself, the unconditional gift that while granting us phenomenality, withdraws from all phenomena. Can this inapparition be thought, then, other than as "promise"? Now this is the thrust of the whole argument which I took pains to show: 'the phenomenology of the Inapparent' is nothing other than phenomenology of promise itself, promise in messianic sense of a structural opening of the world, as the event of disclosure that will henceforth mark all phenomena of the world as a pure gift of being. At the beginning of the world lies promise. The whole domain of language opens in this promise at the very moment one opens one's mouth—even before concept and prior to knowledge—and there is, lo, promise itself! 'That there is promise': this is an inapparent occurrence. It is an event before being; an opening before any predicates. Such promise is "there" even before anything is promised; rather, it is the "there" itself with which each entity of the world presents itself to us in language. One can say that such promise promises itself. It promises all presences in advance before anything being presently present. Such promise promises fulfilment which is not fulfilled in the worldly powers of the profane order, or in the immanent self-presence of our history. In the world that is constituted by "law positing and law preserving violence" (Benjamin), the promise is not yet fulfilled. Hence is the necessity, promised by promise itself: that there must remain a time *to come* beyond the work of death, beyond the violence of history, beyond the gaze of law. This remainder of time is time always *to come*. It comes from an extremity of time, as the *Eschaton* of history, from a future in an infinitive sense of the verbal. The promise of time is this promise: that there will be time after each and every end, because it is at the very opening of the world, because it has begun before any beginning. Only then may there be justice which is not possible within the immanent world of the historical reason. To have time means to have time for justice, time that justice itself demands that everything is not yet finished, that there is always a remnant —a 'not-yet', *Noch Nicht* (Bloch) which is not yet a *topos, being deprived of habitation and a name*, hence is utopian. This is the crux of the messianic notion of the promise and hope that I am attempting to think in the book.

III

The question of history is one of the fundamental concerns of my work. Against the immanence of history which is grounded metaphysically by Hegel's speculative dialectics, messianism rises up with the promise of an eternal remnant of time. Hegel's speculative-dialectical understanding of history, history that is led by its immanent, irresistible force of the negative to a determinate *telos* is only a secularized version of the theological, a theodicy of history. Reduced to an immanent, determinate movement of history, eschatology loses here its tremendous intensity of inspiring the oppressed. In fact the eschatological intensity is here made to serve as finalism in the name of which sufferings, injustice and oppression in the past are passed off as necessary for the sake of, and in sight of its finality that never arrives. Messianism is a refusal of such finalism; instead it evokes, in the name of justice for the oppressed, of an eschatology or messianicity without finalism, an *Eschaton* that would not be part of the immanence of history. Now this is an impossible idea conjured up by messianism: it demands, in the name of justice, an end which is without finality and without end; or rather, it is the end after each and every end; or, even better, it is the hope of an *Eschaton* that must open up time beyond the work of death. It is the apparition, then, which is truly and genuinely inapparent, in the sense that it is not visible *in* the time of time, and *in* the time of history. Messianism is this demand of a wholly otherwise notion of event than the dialectical version of the event that occurs in the immanent plane of history, belonging to human possibility and marked by the violence of law.

In this book I have attempted to think such a notion of the event with the help of Hölderlin. The non-dialectical notion of the event is a "monstrous copulation". Instead of thinking the event as belonging to the speculative unity of the Subject, such event must—in its sudden eruption—bring together in an agonal manner the end and the beginning, hope and melancholy, time and eternity, simultaneously and at the same time. What I am, then, trying to think is not events that are periodic breaks belonging to the metaphysical principle of identity whose unity is guaranteed by the historical becoming of a speculative subject. For me, such an impossible event is the event of the messianic arrival that seizes us while dispropriating us and exposing us to our finitude. That eternity may arrive today, even now, just at this moment when I am reading this line: this possibility is an impossible possibility. Only messianicity realizes this unrealizable, and makes possible the impossible. Messianism de-formalizes time as succession of instants, so that the eternity, which is nothing but an extremity of a radical future, may erupt *here and now*. Prof. Chakrabarti does not see that here is an attempt to think of promise and hope that can't be thought on the basis of Kantian formalism at all. Hope is not here a mere 'future fruit of action' (Chakrabarti). Unlike what Prof. Chakrabarti thinks, hope here is rather a messianic possibility which is the very possibility of justice that demands de-formalization of time. The past injustice that demands messianic justice must conjure up an impossible event that must erupt contra all the believable logic of time as a series of successive instants. That the past may come again and may be lived again in a time to come: this alone may render justice to the past sufferings of the vanquished. It does not belong to the determinate order of the necessary and inevitability of the succession of quantifiable instants. This ethics is the unconditional ethics of redemption. It is redemption that invisibly, *inapparently* passes through history as a secret password, or as a secret index that alone can justify the historical reason. It is in this sense promise is essentially ethical which is to be thought neither on the basis of the Kantian regulative principle nor the basis of Hegelian dialectical theodicy of history. The task here is *not* to construct a theodicy of history (Prof. Chakrabarti laments that I don't event hint at such possibility), but rather to open ourselves to a true eschatology evokes the ethical as delegitimization of each and every attempt of sovereignty in the profane order of world-historical politics. Born out of deepest catastrophe, it is given to the distress of those who are oppressed by history and by the world-historical politics. This thing called 'promise' is also a suspicion. It keeps insomniac vigilance over each triumphal cry of victory that is heard in distance or near. They all for such promise fall short of the absolute and the unconditional. The insufficiency of all that is a human possibility, and *that redemption does not occur at the level of world historical politics*: this is the presupposition of messianism. While this is the source of messianic distress, and this is also the very same source of messianic hope.

IV

Prof. Chakrabarti laments an absence of thesis and absence of conclusions in the book. The serious reader would notice that the notions of "thesis" and "method" are put into question at the very beginning of the book and are re-affirmed at the end of the book once again. Prof. Chakrabarti wants us to philosophize out of Indian context, but he himself never ceases to think in terms of "thesis" and "method"—concepts that have their historical origin in otherwise than "Indian" context. What sad self-refutation! The word "thesis" came from the Greek *Thémis* who is a goddess of law, therefore is connected with *nomos*. A rigorous attention to the problem of "thesis" cannot be extracted from its connection to the problems of law, power and violence. From Heidegger onwards to Derrida and Jean Luc Nancy, the question of "thesis" is therefore problematized. The reader should therefore be left to decide for himself who is more Eurocentric here, rather than Prof. Chakrabarti deciding for us. Similarly the problems of "method", "premises" and "conclusions" need to be interrogated and re-thought. The word *methodos* came from the Greek word (not Sanskrit) *hodos* which means actually "way" or path and not "method" in the sense that has subsequently come down to us during the aftermath of René Descartes (and so also notions such as "premises" and "conclusions"). Prof. Chakrabarti continuously adheres to the fundamental "Western" mode of reading, of argumentation and of method to engage with "Indian" philosophy—modes of argumentation and of method that themselves are already subjected to deconstruction—but he wants us to do what he does, that is, to think out of one's 'lived reality'(Chakrabarti) uncontaminated by "Western" discursive practices. Moreover what does one mean by "Eurocentrism"? One reads Schelling, Rosenzweig, Derrida and Benjamin: does it mean one has become Eurocentric thereby? Is not it that these thinkers themselves, in so many various ways, are confronting, deconstructing and going beyond certain dominant Eurocentrism, which make them infinitely more interesting than a philosopher who philosophizes out of 'lived reality' in a "methodical" manner and by positing "theses" which the European thinkers themselves have gone beyond? One is born in Algeria, lives in France and writes philosophy books that have travelled across the seas and lands: perhaps, this is the most beautiful and profoundest thing about this strange discourse called "philosophy", that it travels beyond, exceeds the given, and welcomes the *Atopos* (namely, the "placeless")—what is not yet lived, and what is not yet (*Noch Nicht*, as Ernst Bloch says). To name such thought, simply because these philosophers lived in a "west" (but thoughts themselves, however, never lived "there" only), as Eurocentrism and to think that to think along with such thoughts would amount to be Eurocentric is a sad judgment coming from such an important philosopher like Prof. Chakrabarti. It is as if thoughts can be possessed by certain people, certain race, certain closed and immobile tradition, a certain pure lived experience. The book, however, opens to another, albeit unfamiliar and strange thought: we may be rather dispossessed by thought, as we are dispossessed by language. Far from being pinned down to the enclosures of a given, identifiable, localizable and determinable "lived" experience and reality, philosophical language dispossesses us and opens us thereby to something new, something yet *to come*, for to live a life itself means to be freed to a journey that exposes us to other shores not yet seen. We are always already in exile, and hope is born in this desert.

In this essential sense philosophy is hope, which is a hope for not yet. It has to pass through suffering and mournfulness, because there is a violence of *topos*: space inscribes itself upon us and forces us to think in a manner that is already there. Against such abuses of history, philosophers like Nietzsche ask us to think in an "untimely" manner, opening philosophy beyond the violence of *topos*. Socrates himself, so unlike Nietzsche in other respects, is the thinker of *Atopos* par excellence, for he conjured up concepts which are not available at that time in that "space", in that 'lived reality'. That does not mean that philosophy thereby becomes an empty air, unless hope itself is an empty meaning for us, unless not yet of hope is pure, vacant, empty nothing. And we know that hope is not nothing, and that justice, even if not yet lived, must be hoped for, despite all mournfulness and precisely because we are mournful being oppressed by the violence of history. This is the connection of mourning with hope that Prof. Chakrabarti cannot think together. We must hope precisely because what we hope for is not yet fulfilled, and precisely because there is a lament in this unfulfilment, calling for an infinite, patient affirmation of a time *to come*, which is I call messianic, not as a particular traditional theological concept but as a philosophical opening, as structural opening of any discourse as such, a 'messianicity without messianism' in Jacques Derrida's phrase. At certain places in the *Republic*, Socrates says to his interlocutors: justice does not exist in the world, for all that seems to exist is suffering and injustice, but that should not be an argument against the necessity of justice, but precisely for it—for a justice *to come*, for a promise immemorially given to us as the very possibility of all and each politics and ethics and of any socially meaningful existence. Justice is the *Atopos*— which is not yet a "space", not yet a 'lived reality' (Chakrabarti)—but it is not nothing, but rather condition of possibility of any *topos* as such, any space as such. This universality is the passion of philosophy par excellence. It is the promise of philosophy as it is the task of philosophy which does not have to be indifferent to cultural-social specificity (being "Indian", to live in "Indian reality") and to be blind to the idiomatic expressions of singularities. It is the uniqueness, the singularity and meaningfulness of the task and the promise of philosophy that it always exceeds the various enclosures of events, existences, thoughts and readings into closed particulars and to the given, fixed, determinate identities. It is the task of philosophy, in the name of the promise of universality, to release the singularity character immanent in all events and existences and which are repressed, by philosophers themselves, into closed particularities determined by the laws of a fixed tradition. Otherwise Plotinus would not have read Indian philosophy, the Japanese should not read Nagarjuna, Schelling should not have read the Bhagavad Gita and Prof. Chakrabarti himself, important philosopher that he is for us, should not read Kant. That they read in such manner, it only shows indirectly what philosophy is: that it is without passport; that it is the fate or rather freedom of philosophy that it travels; and that it refuses to confuse singularity with particularity.

V

Prof. Chakrabarti laments that the book neither has a thesis nor a method (absence of clear premise and obvious conclusion). It indeed does not have one, which has its reason discussed in the book itself.

But that does not mean that everything is in an empty air in the book. Instead of a method, the book puts into a movement certain gesture of reading, a style of disclosure which is phenomenology in a new sense. Phenomenology here is a certain mode of presentation (*Darstellung*): differential presentation of singulars in a movement of constellation, an idea that links this work with the philosophical orientation of Franz Rosenzweig. Prof. Chakrabarti will not find here a conceptually and logically generative principle running through the text to an obvious conclusion. Therefore the traditional methodological principles of distinguishing praxis and theory, content and form, and a progressive movement of knowledge production, deductive or analytic, that concludes with a determinable result: all these are set aside for the sake of a mode of presentation where differential pathways of opening to truth is displayed, in a gesture of repetition, in a constellation or configuration. The reader is invited to read each essay in its own right, in its independence, freed from an overarching "thesis" and yet to see that these essays are different, renewed mode of thinking the same from different perspectives—the question of the promise of time. Therefore it is not a "book" in the sense that the book is a totality of relations with an underlying *hegemonikon* or thesis. Instead, it is an invitation for a discontinuous reading. The rigour of such constellation thinking is a different rigour from the methodical rigour and from the rigour of a thesis. Thus, in the very introductory chapter itself, this kind of rigorous reading, thinking and presenting is named as "way" or "path"—an idea that I borrow from Martin Heidegger and Franz Rosenzweig.

Prof. Chakrabarti refuses to call this book "philosophical", because it does not adhere to his own principles of thesis, of premises and conclusions, of his own specific mode of argumentation. If his specific mode of thinking, arguing and reading is the only philosophical one, then I will be happy to withdraw the book from its claim to be a philosophical work. But who decides and for whom—is it Prof. Chakrabarti? —What is philosophy and who is a philosopher? If it is not yet decided once for all, then it is better to leave this question open, at least for the time being, since there are obviously other modes of rigorous thinking and argumentation without having to have a thesis, a premise and conclusions. But to keep open to such a possibility without closure demands that we really learn to read a book rather than pre-emptying such possibilities by hasty judgments. This means that we learn to open ourselves to the unfamiliar, to the strange, to the not yet space of the book without bringing it back to the familiar self-grounded and self-validating enclosures of thought.

NOTE

1. This text is a rejoinder to Arindam Chakrabarti's review of my book that appeared in *Summer Hill: IIAS Review*, Vol. XVIII, No. 1, Summer 2012, pp. 72-74.

PART IV

FRAGMENTS

11

The Title: "The Divine Names"[1]

I

"The Divine Names": this is the title I have thought for the workshop. If you ask me what this title means, the most convenient way to respond would be immediately to supply the sub-title: "linguistic theories in theology, aesthetics and politics". I, however, feel inwardly that this won't help me either: I don't know enough what is at stake in this title: "the divine names". Yet, I am not inattentive to this specific linguistic mode in which the title comes to appearance and that a title is always a linguistic gesture par excellence. It is a naming gesture, a singular and irreducible linguistic gesture of naming: this giving of a title. In giving a title to an individual, to an event, to a book, we recognize this singularity that lies in our naming, even though we are not always explicitly conscious of this unique way in which we exist linguistically as this linguistic being that we are. Saying this, "the divine names", I am attentive to my use of the definitive article before "divine names", knowing well that generally we don't use the definitive article before the plural. And I am also attentive to my using of the grammatical marker of the plural, as if the names for the divine, even when we think of the divine as only one, can only bear names always more than one. It appears, as though, the divine will never be named enough even when we have always been naming ceaselessly, and even when we always name others —mortals, animals, rivers and constellations—in the name of the divine. As though by a necessary and unavoidable logic that lies in our very naming itself, and in our speaking and writing, we are necessarily beckoned towards that which somehow by definition exceeds all naming and all definition. If for

Hegel and Heidegger, in entirely two different manners of thinking and according to different logics, language means none other than having to confront our death as death, this would mean for me none other than having to confront, at the threshold of our death, what exceeds all naming: the excess of the nameless, the surplus of the unnameable that opens us to the name, to the potentiality of naming as such and naming at all.

Thus I know, and I don't know enough, or, I know without having knowledge at my disposal, what lies as stakes in this title. I wonder what would the title "the divine names" signify for us now, we for who—as for the poet Hölderlin some two centuries back—the divine is in flight, disappeared and disappearing in the lovely blue of the sky, without leaving us with any consolation and salvation? Thus to speak on and of divine names today is something of a risk that one must assume; one thus cautions oneself that it is a prerogative that is no longer "properly" ours, a *hubris* that we must learn to give up, abandon and perhaps even forget. To put the question in a more succinct and forceful manner: why to speak of the divine names today when the divine himself has disappeared, and has been disappearing, without an end of this disappearing in sight, for quite some time now, whose beginning the poet Hölderlin poetized, and then the philosopher Nietzsche philosophized about? It appears as if these two unique mortals in this middle of the epoch that we call "modernity" have borne a knowledge that is excessively tragic, a knowledge that is the vertigo of thought, something like madness or death. No doubt that tragedy is fundamental task of thinking for both these writers in two different ways; in the sense that we call them tragic thoughts. It is not "tragedy" merely in the sense that literature students in college classrooms generally understand it to be, tragedy as a particular literary genre with formal laws and with stylistic characteristics which are provided by Aristotle long ago. It is tragedy in a far more unique sense, as the very thought structure as such that has come to appear in this epochal condition called "modernity"; it is thinking itself that is "tragic" that opens us to this abyssal event of the flight of God or the death of God. I don't need to inform you that the poet Hölderlin went mad at a very young age—I mean "madness" here in the clinical understanding of the term; I also do not need to inform you that Nietzsche too went mad, who has perhaps always been mad from the very beginning. Does this madness have something to do with this enigmatic question of the flight of the divine? As though the divine now manifests itself only under the signature of death ("God is dead", so says Nietzsche) or under the precarious traces of the fugitive God (as Hölderlin poetizes). To speak of divine names today is to evoke names under erasure, as if speaking itself implies today something like confronting one's death and not being able to die at the same time.

To have a workshop on "the divine names" can therefore no longer pretend to be naive. Rather it constitutes a risk whose measure is not yet given in our knowledge, for it opens our thinking to the immense question concerning what constitutes this singularity and this uniqueness that is "today" and "here and now" wherein we find ourselves; for it opens us to the difficult question concerning how to think, and whether it still constitutes a task of thinking for us, of the divine when the divine appears to be disappearing or has disappeared for us, wherein the divine does no longer appear to be a presence among presences in the world. In so far as such is a risk of and for thought, to that extent it also constitutes a task of thinking. Such a risk and task—of thinking and existing—must be undertaken each time anew. This task consists of thinking anew this difficult question, one that is painful and marked by mortality: what does it mean to think and to exist, to poetize and philosophize, to speak and to name in the wake of this event called "the death of God" or disappearance of the divine? Let me pose this question in still another manner: if names are of divine origin, then how to speak today (since speaking involves naming) when the divine himself is supposed to have been disappearing and has disappeared, when he is no longer available to the name, when he is no longer present in our world as presence? I would like to ask myself an even more preliminary question: do our names only name what manifest themselves in our world? Or, in naming, we always name some other thing, another thing, or even otherwise than "thing", the absolutely other or the wholly other that exceeds all presence and appearance? Is naming only a naming of an apparition and of the visible, or rather that, the invisible and the inapparent, without having to pass completely into the visible and apparent, first of all must open the name for us? The invisible and inapparent, far from prohibiting the naming language of mortals, must then be the very possibility of it: it is with which we are always and already open to the world; it is with which language opens us to beings that are manifest in the world, while remaining invisible and inapparent.

It is in the question concerning divine names that this paradox fully manifests itself in its utmost scandal: we name "the divine" who is, strictly speaking, no-one and no-thing and therefore is a no-being; like the way we call death as "death", death which is not a phenomenon like any other phenomenon in the world, but rather that in which all phenomena disappear. And yet we know that death is not a mere nothing: we know well, too well in fact, that people are dying every day, and we know somehow, I don't know how, that we will too die, a knowledge whose certitude no other certain knowledge can measure up to. We know absolutely that we die, and we absolutely do not know when and how will we die. We have names for the divine and for death where each name is a question in turn, a scandal for thought, unbearable and unthinkable thoughts that we never cease thinking in so far as we are still existing, knowing, living and dying. As if each name, especially the divine names—un-pronounceable and pronounced each time—like the name with which we name "death", can only beget a question in turn, for it arrives from the infinitude of the question itself. It shows that there is something infinitude about the very *questionability* itself in all questions. Hence is the proliferation of names without having to receive any answer in turn. A name is a question without answer. The other to whom one addresses in the name, does not give an answer in return, rather another question follows again, interminably and thus refusing to be embodied in the name while opening up the name for us all the while. The divine name and the name for death is a question.

All names, and even so the name of the divine, can thus only be borrowed. To speak a language, to a name someone or something, we must be given to language beforehand, and we must be given beforehand the gift of language. In that sense, all names are borrowed names and we always speak in a language that is borrowed, given to us as gift, without having to be master or possessor of that language. In that sense even what we call the "mother tongue" is never purely and simply "our" language possessed by us in the way that we are supposed to possess territory or a land, as if language is an indivisible, monothetic and nomothetic entity with an essence of its own. The gift of language questions any possibility of our mastery, and dispossesses us from our aboriginal self-identification with any particular given language. Far from possessing a language, as if language were a territory to inhabit, a land to be occupied, a mythic aboriginal identity of self-presence to be possessed, language rather appears to dispossess us, make us non-identical to ourselves and delivers us the desert of no-possession and non-ownership. This is what I take to be the meaning of Heidegger when he says towards the end of his life that language exposes us to our death as death. In language we know somehow without knowing—our death as death—and we know language in a way that we know our death, that is, without knowing what death in itself is. As if an opening to the divine itself can only be a passage of death, that is, to be dispossessed and abandoned by the divine, to be abandoned in the desert of exodus, to be emptied of attributes and predicates of the world. Is this the sense of what Nietzsche says as "the death of God"? As though, naming itself is this passage of death. Names, and if we say "divine names", far from giving us the presence of the divine, rather abandons us, through death, to the inapparent and the invisible without predicates and without attributes. In the pure event of the name, attributes and predicates of the world wither away. It is this pure event of language that opens the inapparent itself to appear. The later Heidegger calls this apparition of the inapparent phenomenologically as "tautology": nothing or no-thing appears apart from the very phenomenality itself. It is phenomenality phenomenalizing itself. Heidegger calls this phenomenology as "phenomenology of the inapparent"[2]. I shall come back to Heidegger, and Heideggerian phenomenology of the inapparent, but before that let me come to the title of the workshop again.

This title, "The Divine Names" is a borrowing one, literally. I have borrowed it from Dionysus the Areopagite's famous work with the same title[3]. He is an early Christian mystic theologian belonging to the 5th century. I have taken up this title in order to open up certain questions concerning what we call "theological" and "aesthetic" and their consequences for re-thinking of the political. As I am speaking, you can't see that I have put here the words "theological" and "aesthetics" within double quotation mark so as to indicate certain hesitation on my part, and also to hint that they themselves are what must now be subjected to our questioning and thinking in this workshop. Borrowing this title from Dionysus the Areopagite, I am not implying that this workshop is devoted to Dionysus's mystical theology, even though it will be a fascinating workshop if we have one on Dionysus himself. Some of the questions that we ask today are the questions posed by Dionysus himself in his own manner, questions very close to what we come to call, after Dionysus, "negative theology". Not taken up without risk—for more than a thousand years and more than seven seas and many lands separate us from him—the title here is to be seen here less as a title of a conference devoted to negative theology, but rather as an indication, as a crypt, as a cipher or a password, or as an index to open up a whole, immense set of questions concerning language that pertain to the "theological", "aesthetic" and "the political". The question of language here passes through like a connecting thread between the theological, aesthetics and the political, weaving a complex texture of thinking that is not immediately visible and popular in our immediate scholarly context. What we must be able to do is something otherwise than thinking these ideas—"language", "theological", "aesthetics" or "the political"—as essentially isolated from each other, and then, as if by an act of violence, yoked them together in an arbitrary manner. Rather what we must be able to do, so I imagine, is to form a constellation of ideas through which a new set of questioning and problematic can be rigorously formulated as much as possible for us by displaying the innermost affinity of these ideas. Hence it could only be called a "workshop", that is, a provisional attempt to formulate something like a new set of questions or problematic that will one day, hopefully, articulate itself in a new research project.

II

I would now like to return to Heidegger once more in order to make visible and explicit the problematic that interests us today and also to illumine the discursive context in which this question appears to us as question. The question that we are asking—that is, how to think this singular linguistic gesture of divine names—is inseparable from the question concerning the closure of what we call, following Heidegger, "metaphysics". In one of his later essays called *Onto-Theological Constitution of Metaphysics*[4], Heidegger understands metaphysics to be constituted in twofold manner of unity: metaphysics is ontologically and theologically constituted. That means, if the question of the divine names is to be thought today at the epochal closure of metaphysics, then it has to be opened towards the outside of the discourse called "theological" in a certain sense. As if, the divine name or divine names can't somehow be thought theologically; somehow it exceeds the discourse called "theological" constitution of metaphysics. From 1935 onwards, Heidegger through his conversations with Hölderlin and Nietzsche sought to open up the question of the name and of the divine name from the theological constitution of metaphysics. Now, I will not dwell here on what is at stake in this peculiarly conducted *Gespräch* or conversation and on its crypto-historical politics. What has remained unthought in the discourse called "theological" is its very innermost presupposition, which is this linguistic gesture of the divine name, the "holy". The holy is what sets apart the world from its foundation. Thus distance or setting apart is what essential to thinking and poetizing outside the epochal closure of metaphysics. The holy, so says Heidegger in the *Origin of the Work of Art* [5], grants first of all the Open by setting apart the world; the poet, listening to the call of the holy, keeps it open in her poetic saying as to welcome the arrival of the holy. It is in this famous lecture called *The Origin of the Work of Art* and in his elucidations of Hölderlin's poetry as well as in his lectures on other poet like Rilke, Heidegger attempts to think the Hölderlinian poetic name "holy" as that which sets apart or distances the divine from the presence: such poetizing, and thinking, unthought within the epochal closure of metaphysics, is what Heidegger thinks to be essentially at stake, not only in the Hölderlinian poetic naming, but in any work of art as such. In the manner that such poetizing is to be distinguished from this discourse called "aesthetics", so the divine name "holy" is to be thought outside the "theological", and what he calls thinking is to be thought beyond the closure of metaphysics, in as much as "aesthetics" as well as "theological" constitute the innermost ground of metaphysics. This much is, then, clear: what could not be thought within the aesthetic expression of metaphysics is poetizing, and what could not be thought within the theological foundation of metaphysics is the holy. This unthought of the holy, far from signifying the immanent self-presence of the divine in the epochal order of world-history, rather hints or beckons us to the Open by setting the world apart wherein the event arrives. Now poetizing and thinking, being neighbours to each other, are these twofold naming that hint or beckons without signification that means, outside the metaphysical language of predicative proposition. This is the Heideggerian idea of *Wink*: it is poetizing and thinking that name the holy without signifying it in the manner of propositional logic of metaphysics. Now you may understand why I have put the words "theological", "aesthetics" and "politics" in double quotation marks, because these terms themselves are to be subjected to questioning and to deconstruction. In that sense, the whole title of this workshop itself is to be put in double quotation marks, or to be marked by a question mark at the end. The post-Heideggerian thinking today takes place in this open site opened by the Heideggerian thinking of the holy, and necessity to think the naming-language of poetry and thinking outside the closure of metaphysics, that means, passing through a deconstruction of metaphysics. If poetizing and thinking has become possible today which keep open the arrival of the holy, which is repressed in the predicative structure of metaphysics, it is because metaphysics has now become *epochal*, that is, finished and completed, terminated and dated.

It is in this discursive context, the contemporary debates on the question of the divine names in linguistic theories of phenomenology and theology and of what we call "negative theology" is to be placed. Thus the debate between Jacques Derrida[6] and Jean-Luc Marion[7], two of the foremost thinkers on this line, and the contemporary concerns, like our contemporary phenomenological attempts to open phenomenology itself to the question of religion and its proximity to the language of poetry and work of art: such debates today can't be understood without the fundamental departure that Heidegger took as a *step back* from metaphysics.

There is, however, another line of thinking that takes seriously the linguistic theories of divine names which is not known and discussed as much as the Heideggerian and the post-Heideggerian discourses that arise in a confrontation with metaphysics. Perhaps the only significant connecting link that I can think of, the connecting link between these two discourses is Jacques Derrida, and perhaps, to a lesser degree, Emmanuel Lévinas. This second line of thinking is singularly pursued by two friends Walter Benjamin and Gershom Scholem, though some of their concerns were already voiced by Franz Rosenzweig who, as we know, deeply influenced both Benjamin and Scholem. The theory of language that Benjamin formulated in his early essays on language, especially in his profound essay called *Language as Such and Language of Man* and later in his *The Task of the Translator*, Scholem is to elaborate much later in his great essay called *The Name of God and the Linguistic Theory of the Kabbala*. I wish I could have discussed with you today these two texts, one from Benjamin and the other from Scholem, for these two texts are crucial for us to understand the issues that really concern us in this workshop. What I can do now is to comment on a small paragraph from Scholem and bring out in my commentary the fundamental stakes of Benjamin and Scholem's theologico-politics. Here is the paragraph: it is from one of the most enigmatic, cryptic essays of Scholem, which is called *On Jonah and the Concept of Justice*:

> The symbolical deed is the just deed. The deed void of meaning is the just deed. To act in deferral implies to eliminate meaning. The meaningful deed is the mythical one and answers to fate. *Justice eliminates Fate.* Isaiah 65: 19-24 not only indicates the elimination of Fate in messianic time but also provides the method of this elimination in the idea of deferral. For the messianic centre of justice is expressed there ironically, since in truth there are not any sinners in messianic time.[8]

Here is the messianic conception of language. We know both from Walter Benjamin's essay on translation and also from Scholem's essay on the linguistic theory of the Kabbala, that their messianic conception of language distinguishes the symbolic dimension of language from the dimension of language as that of signification or meaning. For Benjamin, it is the task of the translator to listen to the symbolic dimension of language that orients any and all language toward the messianic fulfilment, for the true translatability of all translation lies in this symbolic *expressability* of all language as such and not in "this" or "that" expression whose equivalence we try to find in the other language. It is thus the potentiality of language as such, which can't be reduced either to "this" or "that" language, to "this" and "that" meaning, it is this potentiality or promise of language that must be released and emancipated from its enclosure into law or fate. In his *Critique of Violence*[9], Benjamin shows that the essence of violence lies in the means and end relation, a relation that constitutes the very possibility of law. Such violence, which Benjamin calls "mythic violence" is twofold: law-positing violence and law-preserving violence. The mythic foundation of violence is law, whose analogy in the aesthetic domain is the mythic conception of fate. The eternal recurrence of means and end that constantly calls violence to return in an ever new guise: this is the mythic essence of law and is the source of violence. The violence of law strikes us as fate. The mythic-tragic notion of fate is based upon the conception of equivalences between guilt and punishment. Thus, fate too is a mythic conception, appearing as form of law in the legal domain. The language of law and fate is thus the mythic language, one that is based upon the means and end relation; in other words, the language of law and fate is the language of judgment and meaning.

A critique of violence thus must be able to open the mythic circle of law and fate to something absolutely heterogeneous and unconditional outside law and released from the mythic fate. This is the deepest affinity between Benjamin, Scholem and Derrida. The absolute heterogeneity and unconditionality of the Benjaminian conception of the divine violence is that of justice. The messianic justice of divine violence is absolutely heterogeneous to the mythic violence of law. Justice is irreducible and incommensurable to law in so far as its arrival in turn suspends the mythic order of law and fate. As such, linguistically speaking, the messianic conception of justice exceeds all meaning, and all means and end relation by a method of infinite deferral; that means, the deferral of meaning and deferral of the execution of judgment is what constitutes justice. This is what Scholem says in this essay: in the book of Jonah, the divine judgment is passed on Ninevah, but once Ninevah repents, the execution of this judgment is suspended through infinite deferral. If the mythic violence of law erupts from the passing of judgment and its execution, then justice would mean none other than either impossibility of passing judgment or the non-execution of judgment once judgment is passed. Deprived of means-end relation, justice is without meaning: "the deed void of meaning is the just deed", writes Scholem. The language of justice, so says Benjamin, is "pure language", the language of truth where there is no meaning. The divine word of redemption, which is only a symbol and therefore it is symbolic language, is the word without meaning. This is then the messianic conception of revelation that Benjamin formulates as early as 1916: what revelation reveals is nothing, no-thing, and no meaning. It only reveals itself; it reveals revelation itself; it only means itself. It is tautological in this essential sense. This is in fact what the late Heidegger says, following Meister Eckhart, in the name of this enigmatic and paradoxical phenomenology of the inapparent: what phenomenalizes itself as this phenomenology of the inapparent is no "this" or "that" phenomenon, but *phenomenality* itself. It thus occurs only once. It is tautological.

Justice is without meaning by an infinite deferral. It is in this light we now understand the Benjaminian idea of the "politics of pure means", that he evokes at the end of his essay on violence. The politics of pure means is none other than politics without means and thereby without "end". Only a politics without means and without meaning opens justice to arrive, which in turn renders de-legitimate any attempts by any worldly, hegemonic power, founded upon the mythic violence of law, to claim normative obligation from us. Justice is de-legitimation.

In a certain sense, it is no politics, if the meaning of politics is to be understood as means-end relation. It is in that sense Benjamin could say in his enigmatic *Theologico-Political Fragment*[10] that the messianic conception of justice or redemption does not have any political meaning but only a religious one. Politics here is infinitely deferred in the name of the unconditional arrival of justice. Language of this politics of pure means, if we still call it "politics", is the language of pure meaning and therefore, paradoxically, is without meaning, without judgment, without law and without violence. It is an unthinkable idea. Yet, and this is another paradox, essential thinking is preoccupied precisely with the unthinkable. The poetic word of Hölderlin for the divine which he calls "holy" is the word without meaning, because it is a name that opens to the arrival of the unconditional. As such, it is not a word with meaning but *Wink*, a hint or a beckoning that refuses to be totalized in any meaning or in any form of law. It is the non-totality and non-totalisability of the poetic *Wink*, of the divine name as a *Symbolon*, or of the symbolic deed of justice without meaning that is the task of thinking which this workshop today hopes to open towards.

NOTES

1. This was the opening remark in a workshop titled "The Divine Names. Linguistic Theories in Theology, Aesthetics and Politics", held in Jawaharlal Nehru University on March 21, 2014.

2. Martin Heidegger, *Four Seminars*, trans. Andrew Mitchell and Francois Raffoul (Indiana University Press, 2003), p. 80.
3. Dionysius the Areopagite, *The Mystical Theology and the Divine Names*, trans. C.E. Rolt (Mineola and New York: Dover Publications, 2004).
4. Martin Heidegger, "The Onto-Theo-logical Constitution of Metaphysics" in *Identity and Difference*, trans. Joan Stambaugh (New York: Harper & Row, 1969), pp. 42-74.
5. Martin Heidegger, "The Origin of the Work of Art" in *Poetry, Language, Thought*, trans. Albert Hofstadter (Harper & Row, 2001).
6. Jacques Derrida, "How to Avoid Speaking: Denials," in *Languages of the Unsayable*, edited by S. Budick and W. Iser (New York: Columbia University Press, 1989), pp. 3-70.
7. Jean-Luc Marion, *In Excess: Studies of Saturated Phenomena*, trans. Robyn Horner and Vincent Berraud (Fordham University Press, 2004).
8. Gershom Scholem, "On Jonah and the Concept of Justice" in *Critical Inquiry*, Vol. 25, No. 2. (Winter, 1999), pp. 353-361.
9. Walter Benjamin, "Critique of Violence" in *Reflections*, trans. Peter Demetz (New York: Schocken Books, 1986), pp. 277-300.
10. Benjamin, Walter. "Theologico-Political Fragment" and "Fate and Character". in *Reflections*. Edited and translated by Peter Demetz (New York: Schocken Books, 2007), pp. 312-313 & 304-311.

12
Death, Life and Law

I

It appears that in today's world of techno-legality death has lost its existential "meaning". We live in a world that deprives us the possibility of intimation with death in all its existential "earnestness", as Søren Kierkegaard has put it in one of his imagined discourses[1] . These days we are deprived of death. Yet, and this is the paradox, at no other time than ours has seen death everywhere, amorphous deaths, death as banal as "cutting off a head of cabbage or swallowing a mouthful of water"[2], death as penalty which is the gift of the law to us and that strikes us in ever renewed form with its "bloody power over mere life"[3], death as mass technological production, death as useless suffering, countless sacrificial deaths without alter and without a vengeful God. How to understand this paradox: despite the immense manifestation of death occurring everywhere and all the time, death has somehow abandoned us in this advanced stage of technological mass production. Death is everywhere and nowhere. More and more sacrificial deaths occurring without alter and without God, more and more it appears to be the unconditional demand of our time to think a death which is un-sacrificed and unsacrificiable.

This is the reason why in our immediate discursive and argumentative context, the discussions, critiques, debates surrounding on "death penalty" remain so banal, unsatisfactory and superficial, all the time riveting to the same speculation: whether the death penalty deters crime or does not, whether capital punishment—which is the privilege of a juridico-political authority—has power over life or not etc, while fundamental questions concerning the (non)relation of the law and life, between life and death and the question concerning the "status" of death on the historical "experience" of our time, remain unthought and unquestioned. As a result, the question of death remains trapped within the very juridico-political realm from which it is supposed to be released by manner of a thoughtful questioning. A thoughtful consideration will reveal that this difficulty lies in the very unconditional task of opening our historical existence to a death which is to be uncoupled from its fundamental determination of it as sacrifice, even though sacrificial rituals themselves have disappeared long ago, even though the vengeful God seeking blood has departed and has never stopped departing for some time now.

II

This begs the following question: if "death penalty" is authorized to be granted by certain legitimate (we can also say that it is legitimized and legitimizing at the same instance) juridico-political authority, a real confrontation with it should be able to bring into manifestation not only the logic which the legitimacy of capital punishment presupposes but also the logic (or rather the illogic of it) by and in which "life" itself escapes the logic of the law. As it is clear from above that this principle of legitimacy can be none other than the very logic of law itself, namely: the law of economy, understood as equivalences of values, between crime and punishment, between guilt and atonement, between the wrong done and fate striking to the guilty. Walter Benjamin calls this law of economy, which is the law of law itself, by the name of *mythic violence* which is the power of law over life, not over life *as such* however, but over a life as "mere life", life *always already* incorporated and economized within the law of equivalences of values between guilt and punishment. In this justly famous text called *Critique of Violence,* Benjamin shows why and in what manner in such an original guilt-context (original because of its "always already" character) there never takes place expiration of guilt arising from crime. Hence violence recurs, again and again, in the most vicious circular manner, since it cannot imagine an expiration of guilt outside the original guilt-context of the law itself and hence ever new legitimation takes place, once more and all the time, renewing the logic of economy as equivalences of values. From here, at its most intense moment, derives the legitimized logic of capital punishment: since the crime is of nature that is 'rarest of the rare', it can only be expired by rewarding the criminal the equal reward of the ultimate denial of life which is the ultimatum of death so as to bring equivalences of values within the original guilt-context. Here, at an exceptional moment by means of an exceptional measure, the logic of sovereignty asserts its law of economy by reducing life as life *to* life as "mere life". Any good reader of the Benjamin text knows that it is at this 'mere life' that the power of law strikes at, and therefore, this power can never strike at life *for the sake of* life but for the sake of an ever recurring, ever re-circling and never expired guilt itself.

As against it, Benjamin imagines a divine violence where an expiry takes place for the sake of life *as* life. In the instance of taking place of expiry, life is released from the cages of "mere life", from the vicious re-circling of the original guilt context. This instance of breaking through of divine violence also strikes us with death, but not the sacrificial and sacrificed death that has become now as banal as cutting the head of a cabbage but the other death, unsacrificiable and un-sacrificed death of the other. This is justice. Hence justice is connected with death as much as it is unconnected with sacrifice. It is as if, as it were, life *as* life to be affirmed it has pass through a messianic strike of justice which is "experienced" as impossibility of death itself. It is at this moment life *as* life escapes, even if furtively, from the original guilt context of law by a violence without violence, violence without force and without power.

III

Closer to our time, it is Jacques Derrida who has renewed such a messianic notion of justice which cannot be thought on the basis of the law of economy, of the law of equivalences of values which is, as we have seen, the very law of law itself. Therefore justice is not equivalent to law. Justice is the most un-economic possibility; it is not even "possibility" if "possibility" is understood as "capacity" and "mastery" (which is what law founds upon). One can say it is the messianic excess of the law itself.

In a beautiful text called *On Cosmopolitanism and Forgiveness*[4], Jacques Derrida asks us to think of an unconditional forgiveness in excess of the logic of equivalences of values, the later constitutive of the conditioned realm of pragmatic juridico-political negotiations. This forgiveness cannot exhaustively be realized within the negotiated realm of possibilities and conditionalities which often, as we have seen above, uses the logic of ultimatum belonging to the capacities and authorities of the sovereign power.

IV

Thus the debate concerning the capital punishment has to take into account this fundamental question of our time: how to imagine a life, life as life, which is not exhaustively determinable by not just "this" or "that" law but by the law of laws at all, which is the economic logic of equivalences of values? In this difficulty of thinking this life *as* life lies the very difficulty of opening to a death unenclosed within the realm of possibilities and capacities. Such death can neither be sacrificed nor be produced on such mass scale. It will remain the very task of thinking and existing in this damaged world that we are thrown into, and from which we must learn to extricate the very redemptive possibility for a time to come.

NOTES

1. Søren Kierkegaard, "The Decisiveness of Death: At the Side of a Grave" in *Three Discourses on Imagined Occasions* (Copenhagen, 1845), pp. 75-115.
2. G.W.F. Hegel, *Phenomenology of Spirit*, trans. A.V. Miller (New Delhi: Motilal Benarasidass, 1998), p. 360.
3. Walter Benjamin, "Critique of Violence" in *Reflections*, trans. Peter Demetz (New York: Schocken Books, 1986), p. 297.
4. Jacques Derrida, *On Cosmopolitanism and Forgiveness* (Routledge, 2001).

13
Reflections on Hölderlin

One must venture beyond, without reserve and putting aside the spiritual inertia and its forces of gravity, towards the coming of the holy. The spirit too has its force of gravity that pulls it downward into the abyss of its centre. To counter it the mortal must be able to give itself its wing of grace, the wing of light: then perhaps, in the midst of the world's darkening hour, a "philosophical light"[1] will pass through our window sills.

The force of gravity is the force of the centre. There presence concentrates itself into abyss of darkness. The mortals, in terror, flee from it. Whereto?: To oblivion, to the forgetfulness of his destiny, into the noises of the instant, into immediate gratification given in our everyday life. He thus forgets the enduring, what stands out and faces him as the question of his destiny. The mortal becomes untruthful to his truth, refusing to face his responsibility: that is, to venture into the abyss so as to subtract a light that will illumine one day the "default of the gods" arriving.

Only then the mournful "solitary earth"[2] be redeemed and the earth will come face to face with the divine and the tremendous manifestations of the sky, a sky that belongs nothing to any particular nationality, or Europe or Asia. It must have nothing of the spiritual rejuvenation of the soil and blood, nor has it the archaic longing to the once glorified past that will constitute for a nation or a community its historico-political theology. All these manifestations of the political belong to, or to be subsumed to the more originary face-to-face encounter with the forces of gravity and our responsibility to transfigure, in a redeeming act, into the wings of "philosophical light".

Only then history begins anew, and the mortal, once more coming to his responsibility, confronts his mortality and renews himself.

NOTES

1. "Letter to Casimir Ulrich Böhlendorff" in *Friedrich Holderlin: Essays and Letters on Theory*, trans. Thomas Pfau (Albany: SUNY Press, 1988), p. 153.
2. Ibid., p. 152.

14
On the Name

We always name either too much or too little. It is because in the name, language reveals to us a world, or summons a world to erupt that is either too excessive or too impoverished, either too brilliant because of its lucidity or too opaque. Therefore there is always something like danger that adheres in the language of naming. This is true even of the language of piety and of the language of prayer. In each naming there burns a fire. This fire is the secret of the name. It is the element that either breaths life and bestows the glint and the glow and the gleam into the nature of things, or it becomes a consuming wrath, a work of disaster that destroys nothing while giving away each "thing", each "matter" that it names to slow, imperceptible, patient ruination. It melts away even the reticent, recalcitrant named "objects" in the world and gives them over to their truth. This truth in turn will give these named "objects" a new face, a renewed life, a transfigured being.

We always name too late, or rather, we are always too late to name the origin of the world, the origin of being, and the event called "existence". This is the structural condition of possibility of naming as such. This failure to arrive at time, contrary to our habitual thought of it, is not so much an occasion to despair, but rather an occasion to celebrate its blissful melancholy. In the naming, time tests its patience; or rather, by giving us the gift of naming, we are also given over to the time that never ceases testing us and risking us, not "this" or "that" sphere of life but the entirety of our being. In naming, being is exposed to its peril and establishes us as this being whose being is being-towards- its-peril. This peril never ceases to arrive at us each time we name.

We are always too late to name. But to name is still a possibility for us, not so much as power but as loan, a debt, or even a gift. How, then, can we account for this possibility if there would not have been granted to us a time that must remain. The time of naming is thus posthumously born. We only name posthumously. A posthumous time is a time that remains when all time has ended, when the whole world has completed, and history has achieved its end. Strange time it is: a voice in the desert or wilderness, an arrival when all hope is crashed and vanished, when everything is given over to the dissolution which is the truth of everything. When everything passes away because they must pass away, this passing away is at once establishment of their truth.

Philosophy too is a naming. Hence there is a fire that burns in each soul that philosophizes. This fire is a desire, an infinite desire, not so much to grasp the world in the universality of its essence, but more primordially it is a desire nourished by memory of that which has been past immemorially, and which, since time immemorial, has never ceased been past. Philosophy is too posthumously born. Properly understood, this means that philosophy never ceases being taking birth. This is at once an insufficiency, an utter nakedness and exposure of philosophy's nudity, and at the same time a reason of its exuberance that does not allow it to remain sufficient within its being but lengthens its time to what is holy, even if demands the very peril of philosophy itself. Henceforth, philosophy would never be able to open to itself without an inhibition or a hesitation; it would never *be* without simultaneously exposing itself to the peril of its own being. Philosophy must allow, if it is to be possible, the fire to burn ceaselessly at the depth of its existence, even if that does mean its death or dissolution. Above all, philosophy must risk madness. The naming of philosophical discourse is a language that is haunted by the spectre of mortality. Only this radical negation may open this language to its affirmation so that out of negation an affirmation may emerge. We call this affirmation: *beatitude.*

15
Moment

In whose soul the Moment seizes with its utmost lucidity and brilliancy, with its burning intensity as if its presentation can only be approached in a tremor, a shudder, a blinding? It is in the mournful, solitary soul whose entire existence is consumed in the attainment of such Moment, or in the awaiting of it, for only such a soul—whose awareness of his existence is its finitude, its mortality—only such a soul longs, more profoundly than any other, for attainment of such Moment, and therefore towards that which falls outside totality, outside the whole. The rest of the time of life appears to him only as banal monotony of successively passing instants, as barren eternity: against this false eternity, the Moment appears as the eternity of all time together that, in its presentation, appears simultaneously as the arrest of all time. The Moment is the apparition of mortality. The eternity of the moment is the figure of death because it is presentation of the non-presentable, the patience of what cannot endure, the arrest of the fleeting; as the co-figuration or co-stellation of all time, the moment steps outside all totality, in its intensity and blinding lucidity, in the darkness of its presencing.

In the mournful, solitary soul is this experienced more intimately prepared, for by virtue of its mournfulness, such a soul is already attuned to a certain finitude, to the unendurable mortality. Such a soul must be, for that reason, essentially musical, for in music alone—in its pure fleeting endurance of the Moment—the presentation can become a lament. For he who is seized by the Moment is also touched by the limit of language. The experience—or rather its inability—of the Moment enables language itself to step outside any totality, as if language betraying its ability to denominate and designate experience, or the state of affairs of the world becomes music that laments, music that turns into lament.

This is the strange thing about the mortal being: that the mortal, limited by mortality and his ineluctable finitude, is also thereby—by the same gesture—touched by what is beyond. He is the bearer without his capacity to bear what is eternity. He is the one whose very being, by virtue of his very existing, constantly points beyond his own limitation and thereby confronts what is otherwise than himself—the divine and the nature, the animals and the birds, the sky in its various manifestations and what are nourished by the earth. What sustains him is also what consummates his existence; what gives him the power to speak—if speaking is a power—is also what takes the language from himself, in a sort of betrayal, when language itself turns to music, when music turns to lament because it has to speak what is unspeakable, to name the unnamable, to present that unpresentable. Here is the paradox: that eternity is experienced by the mortals only as the figure of death and mortality, the moment at once an arrest of time, the fullness of speech at once a silence, the presentation of presencing is at the same time a darkness, the eternity that is at once momentary.

It is because of that man himself is the paradox of all. He himself is the figure of paradox, and not one paradox amongst others. Oedipus' solution to the Sphinx's paradoxical question lies here: that man himself is the paradox. Neither, at the same time both: divine and animal; neither and at the same time both: eternity and the moment; neither and the same time both: limit and the limited. It is by virtue of this paradox Schelling calls man as the "central being"[1], placed at the boundary, at the abyss of the limit, at the line of decision. In him absolute good and absolute evil are separated by a thin, undecidable line, but at the same time in him alone they are united and possible. Therefore only man, neither animal nor the divine is capable of evil. While in Gods even the violence can not be any less than divine, and the animals can not go beyond their bestiality, in man alone can there occur the *monstrous copulation*[2] of both divine and the beast, but neither of them two alone. Therefore evil is neither divine nor bestiality. It is rather the bestiality becoming spiritual in man, only in him alone. If that is so, he must alone, of his own accord, prepare for the solution of the paradox. Where there is danger, so says Hölderlin, there also lies saving grace.

To sum up with what we began. The mournful person knows, more intimately than others, the necessity of a redemptive eternity which is experienced in him, even in the lament of language, as beatific joy. Unlike what people say: joy and sorrows are not really opposites; they are none but transfiguration of one unto other. Hence the task of mortals: that evil be transfigured into redemption, the danger into saving grace, and sorrows into joy, death into time to arrive. Just like the Eagle's flight, who—as Schelling says— transfigures the force of gravity as mere means into his very flight beyond gravity.[3] If evil is a radical possibility for the mortals—and in him alone it can attain actuality; if death and sorrows are inescapable fate of the mortals; if danger is the place that the mortals are situated, then: we must transfigure them, just like the Eagle spoken above. For that to happen, the mortal must learn to experience of his mortality as mortality; he must assume his responsibility as "central being", because only he can be the most eccentric of all beings.

NOTES

1. F.W.J. von Schelling, *Philosophical Inquiries into the Nature of Human Freedom,* trans. James Gutmann (La Salle: Illinois, 1936 & 1992).
2. Friedrich Hölderlin, "Becoming in Dissolution" in *Friedrich Hölderlin: Essays and Letters on Theory,* trans. Thomas Pfau (Albany: SUNY, 1988), pp. 96-100.
3. F.W.J. von Schelling, *Philosophical Inquiries into the Nature of Human Freedom,* trans. James Gutmann (La Salle: Illinois, 1936 & 1992).

16
From the Other Shore

I

There came once again a phone call from Arindom, an old friend from my student days, now an editor in a well known journal from Assam: 'Satya, write something in our journal for the next issue, something that interests you'. A grant of freedom, a generous grant: freedom to write something, anything, anything that I like; but also a demand that requires a response from my side, a demand in the form of a friendly request from a friend, a demand that one must not leave un-responded. Is not writing, this strange "activity" called "writing", anything other than a *response*, which is the responsibility of the writer par excellence, a responsibility to respond to the other?

"Write"!: not just "write", but write in Assamese, a language that I grew up with, the language that I hardly now speak, write or read. So I must write "something" in a language in which, a long time ago and a long time ago for many years, I had seen the last remnant of sunlight of the evening sky turning dark-red to black behind the shadowy trees and the hills of Assam. So I must write in a language wherein thoughts are not given to knowledge, thoughts ineffable like the breath of flowers or like the murmuring of the sea or like the humming of a distant sea; thoughts that lingers on without being claimed by knowledge in some unknown recesses of consciousness without yet being completely illumined by the light of intelligibility. So I must call to language that elemental depth of existence, that dark intoxicating perfume of materiality that glimmer between shadows and darkness and then disappear; that enigmatic movement between laughter and a smile, between a cry and someone weeping in its utter evanescence, like the evanescent changes of expression in a beautiful face which is all the more beautiful because of its inaccessibility, all the painful because of its unattainablity. So I must write, once again, once again after decades, those words of melancholy where melancholy *itself* rises up from some obscure depth of the soul and laments with the rustling leaves of those trees that are born to wither away in the innermost landscape of my soul. I must write again, once again, those words of ecstasy where ecstasy itself rises up to meet my heart, and I see the autumnal landscape glow with lights from other shores, other lands, other places that I long to visit one day without being able to name them in turn. So I must speak the language of life where even the stones cry out so as to be redeemed from its mutability once my words touch them, move them, like the songs of Orpheus. I must dare to write again, once again, the language of stones, sunsets, laughter of lovers, field of golden corns and the feeling of being vacant in the early afternoon in summer holidays when, the school being now closed, I try to rest in my bed and there and then my soul grows vacant or empty, like the melancholy wind of an infinite desert.

A freedom, but also a demand: a generous freedom and an impossible demand. It is the demand of a response that cannot be evaded or escaped, even though my friend will not bring the force of law upon me if I don't contribute. What kind of obligation, then, is this obligation to respond to a call that does not evoke the force of law, and therefore a weak demand, without sovereignty, and yet, precisely therefore, must not be evaded or escaped at all? There, thus, seem to be demands in life that don't evoke the force of law, demands without law, and therefore being more powerful than the power of law, more forceful than the force of law, demands that don't seize you by hand and in its gaze but rather leaves you abandoned from all force and all mastery. That is why love is always more powerful than law. The face of a child, utterly vulnerable and fragile, utterly to your mercy, is more powerful than the face of a strong man. There is a power of the weak which is more powerful than the power of the strong, for it speaks in the name of non-power or powerlessness. Here we hear the commandment, more powerful than the judgment of law: 'thou shalt not kill'. Therefore, the great ethical thinker of our time, Emmanuel Lévinas makes *commandment not reducible to judgment.* In commandment there is an excess of Good over Being, an excess of ethics over judgment. So it is friendship. A request is always more powerful than a command. Therefore love works better than law, because it is law without law, or a law without works—the infinite worklessness of love that never ceases opening to the other. A response to the demand of love is therefore always more difficult for me, more strenuous, as if I need to draw my last breath upon it, than it is the case with fulfilling the demands of law. A response to friendship, which is responsibility, is always more a responsibility than obeying the law. Law claims my physical life: this is the utmost and the last thing law can claim from me, but love claims my entire soul. I must *dare* love; I must involve in strife with love; I must wage war with love at each moment of my life, at each moment of my day, day after day, years in and years out. This love is sovereign; it is a *true* sovereignty because it works without power, without mastery, without knowledge and without understanding. Like those thoughts, immemorial thoughts—like the memory of a previous existence—thoughts that never arrive at the luminosity of knowledge and therefore is always an excess— thoughts coming to me on a summer afternoon while I wait to take a bath, sitting on the bank of the river that flows nearby my home. And yet, love also is precisely thereby *without sovereignty*: love is always the non-sovereign opening to the other, the non-negotiable life of the soul, the non-conditional soul of my life. In that sense, only in that sense and only in those moments, can life at all be coincident and contemporaneous with love. The moments of this coincidence and this con-temporality can alone be thought as "happiness". Life is happy when the time of life and the time of love coincide and become co-temporal.

II

I must respond. And I must respond without delay. The time of response must be the time "just now" or it is never a response. It is like the time of love: it is "now" or it is never love. The time of happiness too, inseparable from that of love, is the time of "just now", this blink of an eye—at any time, but imminently and urgently, without delay and without "tomorrow". The time of love is the time of the event. "Now" is the event of love, and the event of happiness. It is at just "now", at this absolute moment that there manifests love. Love never manifests itself at any other time if there were no "now", a moment torn from the quantifiable measurement of a homogenous continuum, the eternity of an instant when all words become prayer and all thoughts become piety. We only love and we can only be happy out of the heart of the "now" where eternity throbs like the throbbing intensity of a heart open to the coming other, the beloved or the lover. This "Now" is the mother of love; it is in her womb, love takes birth and is nourished first of all; it is in her womb language in its infancy begins its stutter and stammer. Similarly it is always only "now" that I am happy. That 'I was happy' is a false statement; or at best, an inadequate statement; for 'I was happy' is always less happy than happiness itself. Therefore love is so sovereign, more sovereign (therefore without sovereignty) than law. In his *Letters to the Romans*, St. Paul therefore distinguishes love from law in terms of time, two different times. The time of love is imminent, urgent and therefore absolutely in-exchangeable. It is the time of "now" or never is it love; while law exchanges everyone with anyone under the guise of universality and thereby inserting life unto law. The true time of sovereignty, which is without "sovereignty", is inexchangeable and therefore a non-negotiable demand. There is no love when items of negotiations are already put on the table, or when one loves in order to negotiate the conditioned demands with pragmatic calculations, in the manner that there is no law if there is no negotiation. Therefore responding to the demand of love and obeying the law are two different times. One must quickly respond to the call of love with all the imminence of urgency, for it is a time which is also "no time", because its time is just "here" and "at this moment". *If I don't love now, at this moment, at this place—then there will no longer be time, and there love will no longer be*. This time of the arrival of love marks the end of time, arriving from the extremity of the world: in love we touch the limit of time, the extremity of our life, the border of our existence. There is no love for me if I don't touch the limit of my life, if I don't touch the extremity of my existence, if I don't touch the *eschaton* of history. Only at the end of time can there be a "now", which is the time of love, a time beyond time, time that does not belong to the time of presence. *The end of time is the beginning of love.* Love begins at the end of time. In that sense the time of love is time without time. It is "eternity". Being in eternity alone defines our happiness or beatitude: an impossible thought, for thought begins from it as its condition, like water flows from a source which is like an inexhaustible abyss. Such an eternity arrives "now", or it never arrives. If it arrives tomorrow, then eternity will never be eternity, for such a "tomorrow" or "yesterday" can only be less than eternity and not more. Such a "tomorrow" will only be another time, an extension of today, or carrying the burden of yesterday. Love demands that eternity must come today, just "now", otherwise love cannot fulfil what it must fulfil: it cannot bring the gift of beatitude. In Christian theological interpretation, St. Paul therefore thinks of the eternity of "now"—an imminent, never delaying, urgent and hurried arrival—as the more profound way to open oneself to the divine. As against the time of law that never fulfils the demand of eternity, because it only extends yesterday to today in the manner of quantitative measurement, and thus is based upon exchangeability of times, it is love that alone fulfils the demand of eternity in the non-negotiable arrival of God. God arrives today and just now: hence there is no more time for us to linger on, but to hurry with such urgency, as if the loss of a minute is loss of eternity itself. Love does not know rest, because it arrives under the form of eternity. That we must love and that we must love others who share this world with us: this does not constitute a judgment of law but a commandment of love. This demand and response to this demand is a demand without force, without power, without mastery. It is the non-negotiable demand of eternity itself. Beyond law, beyond force, beyond knowledge, love is faith where eternity cries aloud and makes everything alive—stones, trees, stars, deserts!

III

So I must respond to a non-negotiable demand without delay in the name of love, in the name of friendship, in the name of language that I hardly now speak, write or read. An impossible demand, like the demand of love. What kind of demand does that love impose on me without the force of law?: That I must love the most unlovable! I must have faith when I cannot believe; in other words, I must believe the unbelievable. I must believe in happiness which is unbelievable (can I be happy? Absolutely happy? Blissful like God?); and unless I have absolute faith in love (that love exists!), love will never arrive to me. But we will never know and will never understand that love will definitely arrive, and that there is definite happiness for us. Thus I must love without knowledge and without understanding and without surety. In love I risk my existence; In faith, I wager my soul. I will never know and never understand that God exists. To love on the basis of knowledge and understanding is to enter into the domain of negotiation, into the pragmatic politics of calculable conditions, into the economy of law. That means not to love. To love on the basis of the certainty of knowledge and with "objective" of understanding at hand is not to love, as if one does not love without certain amount of blindness. When one's eyes are open, and *only open and nothing more than that,* then there is no love. When Narcissus' eyes are open, he did not see love nor did he see his beloved; he only saw himself. Therefore there are two different kinds of blindness: one is blind when seeing one does not see; and the other blindness, to see when one is blind. It is this blindness affected the philosopher's eyes when—as Plato recounts it in his *Republic*—coming out of his caves, could not see in the excessive brilliance of the sun. It is this blindness that affected St. Paul on his road to Damascus and transformed him from Saul to Paul.

An impossible demand and an impossible respond! A blind response! It is a response that I have to make in the moments of blindness. I must write in a language that I no longer write; I must read in a language that I no longer read; I must speak a language that I hardly speak: but I must write nevertheless, I must read nevertheless,

I must speak nevertheless—in the name of love, in the name of friendship, in the name of sovereignty without power. And I must respond out of my wound of blindness, without the eyes of knowledge and understanding. Bereft of them, an utter destitute that I am, abandoned and helpless, I must respond without being able to respond. That is true to all other demands that come to me in the name of love, in the name of friendship or by other name, demands without the gaze of law, without force seizing me hand. I must love even though I am not rich enough for it; I must exist even though and even in moments I am so utterly lonely; I must think and philosophize even though most of the time I don't know and I don't understand these thoughts that come to me, from other shore, from other land, from other country. And I love, and I exist, and I philosophize—in blindness, most often without knowing why should I love, without understanding why should I exist, and why should I philosophize. The impossibility of the demand—to love, to exist, to philosophize—is without a 'why'. As if to love, it is necessary to abandon a 'why', to exist without "principle", without ultimate "referent", without appealing to a ground of consolation but not without hope. *This is anarchism, but it is anarchism not of law or of lawless: it is anarchism of love before pity, of justice before law, existence before reason, and philosophy before knowledge.* The blindness of the philosopher, the blindness of the true lover, the blindness of the existent—who is not merely living a bare life—is that other blindness on the basis of which we see life as "life", life in its pure irreducibility to "principles", life that arrives to us, momentarily, like a lightning flash. Such anarchism is not the destructive, violent blindness of law, because it is not founded upon the principle of sovereignty. It is rather the redemptive blindness of justice, the authentic moments of truth, and the eternal moments of beatitude.

IV

So I must respond. I must respond by writing a "something", an impossible "something". It is impossible because it is presupposed that 15 years of my life have not elapsed, that I can name the name (that theological arrogance!), for I will be writing a language where the name is supposed to have been named, and thought can be included in knowledge. It is impossible in still another sense—in not giving me anything as such to write on, so that I can write "something" without prior conditions and negotiations—the ineffable itself will arrive to language. I must write without having to negotiate: a non-negotiable writing! Hence I begun—a blank page before me, without absolutely having no idea at all what I am going to write, without having any knowledge or understanding where all this will lead to, in a moment of sheer blindness, blindness like the way I love the other human beings, like the way I have faith in God, like the way I philosophize and in the manner that I exist this life. And as I love, I exist and I philosophize, this writing is also from the other shore that I have never set my feet on but that has never ceased haunting my dreams from the very inception of my life, or perhaps, haunting me even before "me", before I came to be "me" . I don't have any other idea about love, about existence, about philosophy, other than loving, existing, philosophizing from the other shore. For me, each and every language arrives to me from the other shore, even those first words my mother helped me to utter in the infancy of my existence. They thus bear witness to a failure, an incompletion, an inability, a powerlessness and helplessness: inability to name the name, inability to know my thoughts completely, and even my most fundamental failure to understand myself. But this is also the condition of possibility of my very happiness, of my very life, of all of my responsibilities. If there were no failure, I could never have loved, I could never have philosophized, I could never have been so alive. All the names, even these names in Assamese that have I ever spoken, written and read, all of them are haunted by the spectre of this other shore. This spectre of the other shore has never ceased to haunt me; it inhabits each word that I utter, each time I love someone, each time I feel I am alive. Hence this response too, starting with a staring like a blind man at the blank paper for half a day—without the grand light of knowledge—must arrive from that other shore, haunted and blind—like love, like philosophy, like faith—but here and now.

17
The Infinite Speech

Fragment 1. *The Immemorial*

Why is it so difficult to speak of things that one loves most, of a happiness or joy that strikes one most? As though in such profound experience, the richness of experience must bear the poverty of language, depriving us the very possibility of speech, stripping us nude and wholly bare. As though the moment consumes itself, and in speaking of it or in remembrance, the moment may only appear a *passé*, an instance that has fled at an infinite speed like the arriving and passing of a comet in the night's sky. As though between us and our own experience lies there an irreducible split, an interval not to be bridged; though the very possibility of speech, given to us mortals, can arise only from this yawning abyss. This instance of time, opening the heart of finitude to the infinite, refuses to be embodied, without remainder, in the *logos* of the world. Thus the world remains *to come*, always *to come*—out of the very wound of its mortality. The birth of the world opens up in that abyss of *diachrony* that is our mortality.

That's why our profoundest experience is so paradoxical. It is at once full and empty—where plenitude derives its sense from poverty and poverty from plenitude—at once full of having to name and the impossibility to name, an inscription of an interval which effaces any inscription of time. A diachrony that *spaces* between times, and hence is otherwise than time: it is mortality itself, inapparent in time, appearing only as this distress in this *setting apart* of time from itself. It is existence at the limit, existence that has *ex-sists* ecstatically, fleeting in its arrest, like the images of past happiness or dreams of a beautiful future world. This instance is the noon of the day that, reaching its fullness, impoverishes all the attributes and empties out all the predicates of the world: such is the abyss of this noon. Therefore speech, even when one speaks of the present and of presence, has an essential relation to "it was", or "it happened", "or I was happy", even though one speaks of present happiness. This is why we always think of happiness in relation to distant times in the linguistic formulation of "once upon a time" with which fairy tales begin. *All speech is fabular, fable-like, and fabulous.* All speech on human experience originates as fable; or, rather, fable is the origin of speech. "Once upon a time" is not a time as one particular instance homogeneous with a present "now", but a time that precedes all times, a time before time, a past before past, more distant than any distance and nearer than the near. A fabulous time of fables: "once upon a time", an immemorial "once upon a time", an excess of time over memory. This immemorial is the origin of all memories. The immemorial *fables* (in verbal sense) us as mortal existence open to the world, open to the divine, to the animals and birds, to the elemental forces of the world, to the solitary earth and the blazing sky of eternity.

There is, then, something fabulous and fable-like about our happiness. Our happiness is fabulous: prodigious, extra-ordinary, fantastic, marvelous and unbelievable. What has happened, could not have happened!: astonished, so we think. Our happiness takes its time from the eternity of the immemorial when everything is "once upon a time": fabulous, fabular, and fable-like. The astonishment of happiness—happiness that astonishes us, surprises us, seizes hold of us, catches us unaware—has a profound relation to a time that does not belong to the world of presence: it is either a world past, so immemorially past that all beginning must begin with it, or it is a world always *to come*, unfinished and unfinishable, unfinished at each moment of the end of the world. The world is thus without beginning and without end. It is happiness, unconditional happiness that opens to this world that has *always already* opened itself to what is always *yet to come*. At the instance of its end, the world begins anew. At the instance of the end of the world, there is a little bit— just a little bit, almost nothing and not yet absolutely nothing —of the world still left. Happiness, born out of catastrophe, is the experience of this recognition of the remainder of the world: the world is still remained, is still remaining, will still remain. What the immemorial "once upon a time" intimates us with is this messianic remnant of the world.

This relationship of time with happiness intimates in most ancient fairy tales and imaginative discourses, from Plato's notion of *anamnesis*, of primordial remembrance to Proust's *Remembrance of Things Past,* in Rousseau's evocation of existence in nature and in the Judeo-Christian idea of the paradisiacal existence before the Fall. They speak of a remembrance of an infinitely past, immemorially past happiness that is "once upon a time", a remembrance of fulfilling time, when time itself was full in such a manner as if we can *speak* of happiness as *remembrance,* as though the very opening structure of temporality that opens existence to happiness and happiness to speech can only be—by a logic unforeseeable and ineluctable—that of "once upon a time". To speak of "once upon a time" is to speak of a time *one* with being, when time is not yet experienced as separated from being, when it is not yet experienced in the distress of being's disjunction from its time. To be one with time, to be one with everything, to be one with the created mortals and the divine: this is Godlike bliss and happiness, the paradisiacal existence that once was. Thus Hölderlin's Hyperion speaks to Bellarmin in Hölderlin's text: "*es ist ein Gott in uns, sezt' er ruhinger hinzu, der lenkt, wie Wasserbache, das Schiksal, und alle Dinge sind sein Element. Der sey vor allem mit Der!*"[1] To be one with all elements, with one's fate and destiny, with all directions is Godlike. To say "I was happy", in *remembrance,* is to say in gratitude of a past happiness; it is to say "thanks I was happy" and that "there was a time when life was not yet damaged". Gratitude thus always has certain relation to remembrance of this immemorial past. To say "I am happy" is never happiness enough, and thus it is to be ungrateful to happiness. Gratitude and happiness—gratitude for happiness—has the relation with a past remembered, a childhood when the harvested fields of autumn were filled with fairies who spoke to the child in a speechless speech, or the enchanted dream of the youth to be with the young girl he loves, whose house he passes by looking at the window in order to have a glimpse of his beloved.

In that sense our adolescence is not immaturity but our exposure to the un-communicable, the unnamable and the unsayable that overwhelms us. It is the experience of abundance that is the lack of the name; it is the fullness and plenitude that is the abyss of speech, for it is that point which henceforth the growing adult will seek to erase in the name of "wisdom". It is from this abyss of the fullness arises the birth of speech. It is the infancy of speech which is not yet speech—which experiences, for that matter, the lack of the name—is that which overwhelms us with its excess of time over memory, with its excess of affection over knowledge, with its excess of life over the ego or the subject of experience. To say "I was happy" is to say of an experience which one never experiences; it is to be grateful to none, to nothing in *particular*, or rather when there was nothing in particular to be happy, when no particular ego—the cognitive bearer of experiences—has yet emerged. Such a mode of existence without *arché,* without principle or reason, is—in a profound sense—*anarchic.* Thus Angelus Silesius says:

> The rose does not have a why; it blossoms without reason/Forgetful of itself, oblivious to our vision.[2]

This stillness of our speech is fullness—"without a why". Franz Rosenzweig therefore calls silence "perfect understanding": "There is a silence here that is unlike the speechlessness of the primordial world that has no words yet, but a silence that no longer needs words. It is the silence of perfect understanding"[3]. There is a silence that is not an emptiness of names, but the completed name—of bliss complete, of happiness paradisiacal—for which one is grateful silently, in completed understanding. How to name this silent fulfilment of names? How to name the silence that has completed the name, and hence rested in forgetting? It is as if to be grateful, to remember each time for past happiness is to remember the immemorial; it is as if to name and to speak each time is to speak the silence that is the completion of the name. How to remember the forgetting? How to name the silence, the completion of the name? This is the impossible demand of speech, out of gratitude to the paradisiacal past happiness: remember the immemorial so that there may remain what is *always to come*!

Fragment 2. *The Remnant of the World*

There is, however, a certain barbarism that lies in our desperate attempt to name the unnamable, in our desire to exhaust the unnamable in the name. It is barbaric name the horror of unnamable at the destruction of the name. Here Adorno's saying that it is barbaric "to write poetry after *Auschwitz*"[4]—becomes meaningful. It is not the barbarism of being ungrateful to the paradisiacal existence of the past when the name is not yet a name, when the name names the unnamable out of gratitude; but the rather opposite: the unspeakable destruction of the name that would have been grateful to the unnamable; it is the horrible destruction of the unnamable. There is an unspeakable violence and barbarity in the destruction of the unnamable; there is violence in totalizing the unnamable in the name, even if that be in such a fragile discourse as poetry. One must leave, out of respect and gratitude for the unnamable, to its own provenance, and not to assume the theological violence of naming the name itself. Adorno's saying, therefore, has two senses, incommensurable to each other: on the one hand, there is a violence and barbarity in totalizing the unnamable in the name (one must leave the unnamable to its own provenance); there is also the other violence, which is to presume today, after *Auschwitz*, that there is still a language that from a distance, undamaged by violence, can poetize the experience of the horror. To write poetry, that means to name—what is poetry if not naming?—after *Auschwitz* is impossible because the unnamable, to which the name is born grateful, is destroyed. To name after *Auschwitz* is to presuppose that there is still the unnamable to name, to presuppose that which is our gravest irresponsibility.

Yet there is poetry after Auschwitz, but then such poetry is no longer "poetry" in the classifiable sense of the philosophical discipline called "aesthetics". Paul Celan's poetry is poetry in this sense. It is no longer poetry; it is no longer aesthetic representation of human experience. It is no longer simply the naming discourse that presumes to names the unnamable. It is poetry of the survival, the remnant of naming, the leftover of what could not be named. Thus these two incommensurable statements are to be affirmed at once: we must not write poetry after *Auschwitz* (it is irresponsible, "barbaric"); but all that saves us today and all that salvages the very possibility of naming at all is nothing but this remainder, this remnant of speech that is poetry. Thus Paul Celan's poetry is not just poetry of remnant but remnant of the naming speech of mortals, the survived words—broken, damaged, worn out—of what has remained.

Thus the demand of speech, when speech is impossible and barbaric, is the speech of the damaged life. It is the melancholic speech at the destruction of the name when there no longer unnamable to be named out of gratitude. The ethical task of the naming, when the name is born out of damaged life, is to think of redemptive happiness, or the happiness in redemption, happiness of the coming without violence and without destruction, without objectification and reification. Therefore all utopian tales, of imaginary happiness and beautiful world, has this necessary relation to the future. The demand of the utopian world is an essentially ethical demand, born out of damaged life, incessantly to keep open the still remainder of the world. Born out of catastrophe, the name is the sparkle—dimly seen, standing against the immense abyss of darkness—of that messianic hope for redemption for mankind. In this melancholic name, broken and damaged, the mortal hope survives. As if to write poetry after *Auschwitz*—like Paul Celan's poetry—is still keep open the remnant of the name, unnamed and unnamable in the historical destiny of what has been. To speak is to wait for the other from the heart of time that transcends itself, like language addressed to the other who is coming from the extremity of time. Therefore naming, writing poetry—that is to address the other, to respond to others who are not yet born—is our gravest responsibility, responsibility to hope against all hopelessness, to salvage that little sparkle against the night of oblivion.

Fragment 3. ***The Infinite Speech***

To speak is, thus, ineluctably to come across the fundamental aporias of what is called "experience": one must be able to speak of a disappearance while still alive; one must speak of a limit that is without memory and without time; one must speak to tease out that little remnant of sparkle on the verge of its disappearance; and to wait, while speaking, for the other, in hope and in promise, on the threshold of catastrophe. In other words, the paradox or aporia is the aporetic relation between two times: all speech, while belonging to the time of presence, originates from an event of temporality that exceeds all presence and absence, all memory and all cognition, as if language—this giving us of the sense of the world—can only a surviving of a time that has never belonged to presence and absence. A radical heterogeneity, an absolute outside of the world—not just another world— must give this world to us before hand, in a time preceding all memory and all cognition. An invisible exteriority, whose invisibility is not a mere privation of the visible, must have *always already* opened all possible interiority which constitutes our world of meaning and knowledge. As though a radical non-contemporeinty with all that is presence must have already opened the very possibility of contemporeinty itself on the basis of which we understand this world as "world". It is only basis of the immemorial non-contemporeinty alone can there be a time that is to remain after all destruction and catastrophe. The indestructible speech it is, speech that is to remain after all end; infinite speech it is, persisting when nothing any more to persist. The infinite speech: speaking after all conclusions, beginning after all end. The infinite testimony: to bear witness when there is nothing to bear witness anymore.

The infinite speech arrives with this unconditional demand: that we must henceforth speak, only from now onwards, and precisely now when there is nothing more to speak; that we must speak when speaking appears no longer possible, no longer a "possibility" or a "capacity" for us. Speak—without capacity and without possibility: is the infinite speech. Who can escape this unconditional demand? All creative thinkers, philosophers and poets, creative artists confront this fundamental, essential demand of speech: to speak when there is nothing more to speak, or to speak when language is not yet a possibility or capacity for us. This is why speaking is so inextricably tied to our finitude. Who is the mortal that can avoid this double demands that speech impose upon and free us towards language? On one hand, to speak is to say everything absolutely and completely, with a generosity without reserve and without remaining anything to say anymore; yet to speak is also to have the possibility to speak again and thus not being able to speak without an irreducible remnant, without what is radically outside knowledge, speaking one more time and *ad infinitum*. To speak is to share the knowledge that one has in one's disposal, to make knowledge communicable and comprehensible; but speech—by beginning anew and beginning without end— makes the speaker unknown to oneself, or even makes the speaker monstrous. Traversing through a finite existence of a finite speaker, the infinite speech makes the speaker non-contemporaneous with herself, an enigma to herself. "Was it me?": so the question murmurs monotonously in her deepest solitude, in moments when the din of the world dies away and a mortal confronts the question of her destiny, when her own existence becomes the most enigmatic riddle. The question recurs–like the billowing waves of the infinite ocean, surging forth—haunting to the mad point of obsession: "was it me?", as if oneself, one's existence, one's death does not belong to oneself ; as if it is possible to die and exist, to suffer the eternal despair and to burn in joy only as another, only as other; as if it is possible to exist only by not knowing enough of oneself, by not yet seeing the abyssal source of being, only by the distraction of a gaze turned away from what is one's truth about oneself. Henceforth something really strange may happen. One remembers the story of Coleridge's *The Ancient Mariner*: like the one whose existence is called into question by the fact that he exists, or whose experiences demand speech by the fact that experiences do not belong to the communicable, the demand now arises—like the one suffering from compulsive disorder —to keep on incessantly speaking after every after, to continuously repeat compulsively of the event that has happened outside time, as if only by the incessant speaking-repeating would redeem, or bring salvation to the condemned man. He speaks henceforth, not so much to speak about "something" or "someone", but only so that there may remain speech, so that one may speak without end. This is his only hope, the hope for an infinite remainder of speech to come. Kafka writes, and he writes compulsively, because his hope comes with the demand that writing must continuously open spaces and burst out time from all enclosure of immanence. He writes so that writing may remain: this is his salvation, his messianic hope.

Fragment 4. *Originary Mourning*

How to speak the truth of the event, when the condition of possibility of speech is simultaneously a turning away from the event so as to speak it? In essential speech, there is a simultaneous turning towards and turning away from the event with which our speech is obsessed. On one hand, speech turns towards the event that has, in a certain sense, either already happened or happening still; but, on other hand, speech turns away from the event, from the purity of the event, from the fire of its manifestation, in order to address to the others who are still coming from the purity of the future. Thus the event of truth makes speech necessary and impossible at the same time: it makes language a necessity, almost a compulsive necessity and yet impossible. Speech must bear the truth of the event, unbearable truth, truth of the event burning in the blazing landscape of manifestation; but speech must also, so that it may speak to us at all, turn away from the event so to make it communicable, universal, "common". It must take its birth from the source of the immemorial, from that which is outside memory and in-excess of affection beyond the subjectivity of the speaker; but speech must also be able to open up the immemorial to the pure event of what is always to come.

Speech must keep truth—like the Egyptian Pyramid— and maintain it in an eternal act of remembrance; in the dark depth of secrecy, must speech keep alive the singularity of the event. But, speech is not speech if it is not, in a sense, universalizable. As though, all speech takes its singular birth from an originary source of the immemorial only to efface it or transform it into the universality of communication. There is no speech that does not take birth from the immemorial, but the immemorial, while inhabiting in all speech, remains the unspeakable par excellence. Giving us the gift of presence, the immemorial withdraws itself so that speech becomes possible for us, so that we don't turn into ashes in the blazing landscape of its manifestation. As if to speak the event is not to speak it, to efface it beforehand, not to be there at the event. All speech is therefore posthumously born: the immemorial must precede it, always, so that speech may arrive to the mortals. Happening outside the self-presence of the "I", all speech is opened by the structural condition of "once upon a time". In that sense, all speech—not just "this" or "that" speech but the very potentiality of speech as such—is fabular, fabulous, and marvelous.

To assume speech is thus the gravest, heaviest task. It is to speak at that point when there is no point to assume for speaking, when there is no one to speak. At this point, when there is none, speech emerges. It emerges by bearing the anguish of unbearability, the pain of maintaining the lack of the name, the lack of speech itself. Henceforth what it must speak is none other than this very lack of speech, the very absence of the name, the very emptiness. The impossible!

> *A boy, adolescent, passes through the harvested field of an autumnal evening. The harvested, golden corns lie gathered here and there by the farmers who have left for home, and the birds, silently flying back home in the eternal sky, share the anguish of the dying sun. The sky itself, illumined by the last amber of the day, has grown mute. The boy came home, and since then, as if infinity of the days have passed and infinite times the sun has set, infinite times the birds have come home in autumnal evening in infinite numbers. The boy too has passed his adolescence, his youth and his manhood and himself has become the evening sun of the autumnal evening; his birds too have drunk the wine of youth and have now passed away silently in the sky. But what has happened that day, that evening in him outside him—with the sky, with the autumnal field and with birds —have not stopped happening in him from then onwards, and has recurred incessantly, thenceforth, every evening the same evening coming and repeating with a repetition that is infinitely the same dying sun, the same birds mute with*

anguish, the same harvested field of golden corn. Henceforth he has carried, without being able to, the impossible and unnamable. Henceforth he speaks and names, incessantly that has become his obsession, only to speak one and the only thing that he would have liked to speak, the one and the only thing he would have liked to share with others (that includes not only humans, but also animals and birds and with the elemental forces of nature) to name to unnamable, to speak the unspeakable, to share the un-shareable enigma. He wants to speak the truth of a secret that he can not bear, and that he bears it in this impossibility, in a patience of time from where time takes its patience. Henceforth he speaks, obsessively and incessantly, in an irremediable compulsion that comes from elsewhere—and he speaks to the animals and birds, to the humans and to the silence and thunders of the sky—speaking everything so as not to speak the only essential he would liked to speak, the single event that has happened without happening, the only and one important event of his life which he bore witness, and which he can not testify, which has thenceforth grown silent within him more he spoke. He grew more solitary more he binded himself with others. He has henceforth carried a secret of a distressed waiting which has deprived him of his agency and selfhood. Henceforth he is eternally on the way, a pilgrim on this mournful earth ; his distress is the distress of the eternally awaiting one, whose solitude has no commonality with the world . It is the speech of the eternally awaiting one, who is yet to be born, waiting for the birth of the world. Henceforth he shares everything with everyone, but an essential silence grew with every speech, and in every speech there resonated that humming of that distant world, nearer than anyone and more distant than anything. In each murmur there resonated that melancholy of the sun and the tears of the golden corns, as if what has befallen on him that day is the melancholy of speech itself, the melancholy of the name.

This mourning is the origin of speech, and for that matter it is not all that is communicated in the mediated language of concepts. Walter Benjamin in a beautiful essay[5] shows how such a profound mourning intimates the very contiguity of beings in such a manner that it intimates us with certain muteness. Mourning makes nature mute. As though there is in all speech a veil of unspeakable mourning; as though language is open to itself by a movement that is not simply "linguistic": It is the hollow of a cry that is too early to attain cognitive truth and too late to remain in itself as its ineffable essence. Like a fable, it beckons toward that which is in-excess, unsaturated, indemonstrable.

Fragment 5. *Abandonment*

Madness watches over the one who speaks the essential language of solitude. Hence, as Aristotle famously says, that a melancholy—melancholy to the point of madness—haunts geniuses, namely those who create, for what is thinking if not thinking the limit of thinking, thinking at the limit, thinking the unthought, the vertiginous unthinkable? What may this limit of thinking be otherwise than madness? If there is no thinking without this constant "solicitation to madness", one cannot thereby say the philosopher is simply mad. Hence is the necessity, as Schelling says so beautifully, to allow oneself a regulated form of madness.[6] This regulated madness can only be attained by an infinite act of mortification or abandonment. Here is Schelling, quoted by Martin Heidegger:

> He who wishes to place himself in the beginning of a truly free philosophy must abandon even God. Here we say: who wishes to maintain it, he will lose it; and who gives up, he will find it. Only he has come to the ground of himself and has known the whole depth of life who has once abandoned everything, and has himself been abandoned by everything. He for whom everything disappeared and who saw himself alone with the infinite: a great step, which Plato compared to death.[7]

Thinking abandons us. In essential thinking the worldly attributes undergo mortification. We, thus, do not think on the basis of our "possibility" or "capacity" but on the basis of being abandoned (of being banned, being exiled, being left outside the thought's possibilities, or possibilities of thought), as if, as it were, thinking is the gift of death. The essential language—of poetizing and thinking—partakes in this essential gift. There is no partaking in the gift of language without being abandoned by ground, by the foundation of things. In his later works, Heidegger attempts to think the notion of "event" precisely in relation to this idea experience of abandonment, of being abandoned by Being.[8] To think is to be abandoned by its ground, abandoned by possibilities: this is the freedom, rather than fate, which calls us at the closure of the Occidental metaphysics to make a new inauguration, outside metaphysics, possible. It is possible at the closure of metaphysics to hearken to the call of Being in poetizing and thinking. The language of such poetizing and thinking is not the categorical-conceptual language of metaphysics but the infinite speech of abandonment, the speech of the rose that exists "without a why". The essential speech-thinking, unlike the categorical-conceptual thinking of metaphysics which is without language, is this infinite speech arising from the heart of the finitude of the world, non-totalizable and always in-excess of what is presently given. Called by what Schelling calls "un-pre-thinkable", thinking thus remains open to what cannot be thought, the un-thinkable that must give—always and already—the very possibility of thinking for the mortals.

Such a speech-thinking is fundamental to Martin Heidegger's later writings as much as his *Being and Time*. That the mortal may speak at all has an essential relation to his mortality as mortality. Man is not primarily the animal who has the additional rational capacity of speaking, but that he is what he is from the essential ground of his being, that is, its nothingness. Being *phenomenalizes* itself as this essential nothingness of *Dasein*. The mortal is the being who speaks, who alone can speak, not because he has added rational capacity for speech, but because in speech the essential finitude of Dasein *phenomenalizes* itself. The impossible possibility of death for the being whose being is being-towards-death is, therefore, at the same the very possibility of language as such. If *Dasein* decides not to speak, or to be silent, or finding it impossible to speak, it is only in so far as speaking or language is possible for *Dasein*. Only because *Dasein* speaks, may he thereby remain silent. The essential possibility of speech for *Dasein* is the very possibility of *Dasein*'s being, that is his essential mode of being as this being-toward-death. The essential connection of language with death is the existential character of Dasein's being-towards-death. *Dasein* speaks on the basis of a non-capacity and impossibility of finally not-being-able to assume and appropriate one's own being.

I, however, wonder whether language is unique to man. Where then one decides on the relationship between *Dasein* and animal, man and beasts or birds and thus between language of man and the cry of animals? With this—and Jacques Derrida shows for us with his acute sensitivity[9]—the Heideggerian neat distinction between fundamental ontology and regional ontologies, between the existential and the categorical[10] becomes undecidable. Can it then be said that language is the basis on which one can distinguish man from animal? Or may it not be otherwise: that language is the opening-spacing of *Dasein* with what is other, even non-human, animals and beasts and birds, plants and elemental forces of nature? It may be that *Dasein* speaks in so far as he bears witness the other's death whose death is not a possibility of impossibility, but—as Lévinas and Blanchot say—"an impossibility of possibilities". Dying is, thus, never primarily that of oneself dying, but it is always, foremost, the dying of the other. In that sense, speech is an infinite response, an infinite responsibility to the other. It is always on the basis of other's death that we may speak of death. This is the Levinasian complaint against Heidegger. What is essential to language, so Lévinas argues, is not its existential-apophantic disclosure of Being, but that of an infinite response, borne out of an infinite responsibility to the other. As such, such infinite opening exceeds the Heideggerian distinction of the existential and the categorical.

The infinite speech is this infinite responsibility to the infinite other. Opening from the heart of finitude, this speech transcends itself, opening itself to the other who comes from the extremity of time.

NOTES

1. Friedrich Hölderlin, *Hyperion* (München: Deutscher Taschenbuch Verlag, 1997).
2. Angelius Silesius, *The Cherubinic Wanderer*, trans, Maria Shrady (Paulist Press, 1986), p. 54.
3. Franz Rosenzweig, *The Star of Redemption*, trans. Barbara E. Galli (University of Wisconsin Press, 2004), p. 313.
4. Theodor Adorno, "Cultural Criticism and Society" in *Prisms*, trans. Shierry Weber Nicholsen (The MIT Press, 1983), p. 34.
5. Walter Benjamin, "On Language as Such and the Language of Man" in *Selected Writings, 1913-1926*, Vol. 1, eds. Marcus Bullock and Michael W. Jennings (Cambridge, Massachusetts: The Belknap Press of Harvard University Press, 1996).

6. F.W.J. von Schelling, *The Ages of the World*, trans. Jason Wirth (Albany: SUNY Press, 2000), pp. 102-104.
7. Martin Heidegger, *Schelling's Treatise on the Essence of Human Freedom*, trans. by Joan Stambaugh (Athens: Ohio University Press,1985), pp. 6-7.
8. Martin Heidegger, *Identity and Difference*, trans. Joan Stambaugh (New York: Harper & Row, 1969).
9. Jacques Derrida, *Aporias*, trans. Thomas Dutoit (Stanford: Stanford University Press, 1993).
10. Martin Heidegger, *Being and Time*, trans. John Macquarrie and Edward Robinson (HarperCollins, 2008).